Contents

Living with stress

a Consumer Publication

Consumers' Association
publishers of **Which?**
14 Buckingham Street
London WC2N 6DS

a Consumer Publication

edited by   Edith Rudinger

published by   Consumers' Association
publishers of **Which?**

Consumer publications
are available from
Consumers' Association
and from booksellers.
Details are given at
the end of this book.

© Consumers' Association March 1982
reprinted September 1984

ISBN 0 85202 208 5
and 0 340 27486 7

 Printed in Great Britain by
Page Bros (Norwich) Ltd

Living with stress

One man's mild stimulation from life is another man's intolerable burden. What is severe stress to me, may be no more than a tiresome or niggling incident to you. The degree of stress is determined not only by external events but also by how a person perceives the events and responds to them. There are few absolute sources of stress: the interaction between a potential source of stress and the person's own attitudes and vulnerabilities determines whether a situation is experienced as stressful.

In general, stress refers to pressures on an individual that are in some way perceived as excessive, or intolerable, and also to the psychological and physical changes in response to those pressures.

There is a close link between processes in the body and processes in the mind. Stress influences both of them, and some illnesses are regarded by some doctors as specifically stress-related. Stress can be the cause of some illnesses, it can make others worse, and is involved in the mechanism of yet many others.

So, not only does reducing stress to tolerable levels lead to a more consistent or greater sense of well-being, it also reduces the likelihood of some physical illnesses.

It is not easy to lessen stress when a person faces a whole range of problems rather than one identifiable difficulty. Moreover, people under a lot of stress are less able to cope. This in turn leads to more stress and less ability to cope – and a vicious circle sets in.

A modicum of stress is part of life, and is not necessarily always bad. Even joyful events, such as a marriage, a birth, a new job, can be stressful because of the changes they entail in the person's life. So, the key issue is not how can stress be avoided, but how can it be coped with to advantage. Stress can sometimes even help to develop latent resources.

Useful organisations are listed throughout the book with the symbol ❍ and can also be looked up in the Index. When writing to an organisation for information, please enclose a stamped self-addressed envelope.

The ages of man

Stress can occur at any age; no one is too young or too old to feel its effects. It is most likely to occur in situations where adjustments are needed.

when young

Infancy is not generally regarded as a stressful time – by adults. But just because people tend to forget their own babyhood, it does not mean that it was stress-free. The infant is dependent for his gratification on others, who are not always kind, and has not yet learned to cope with his own raw reactions and frustrations.

A small child has to contend with things such as the arrival of a new baby, being restrained, fear of the dark, being left alone, teasing, not being given things, having to share, and being chastised.

One of the models that people take into adulthood, however much they may consciously wish to get away from it, is that of their parents' attitudes and their own experience as a young child in relation to the mothering and fathering they received. Coping with stress is learned from childhood onwards – and parents can help to teach children how to cope. By putting her arms around a distressed child a mother does more good than by shouting and scolding, as often happens. People who have not been treated in an understanding manner by their parents will not find it easy to be understanding parents when they themselves have children.

With busy, working parents, children may feel left out and that they have no one to talk to about their own problems.

School brings with it the need for major adjustments, not only to discipline and teachers but to other, unknown, bigger children. Unhappiness at school or fear of bullying often leads to stress.

More specific problems include lack of achievement at school, especially if the parents consider it due to lack of ambition or application. Even being a gifted or precocious child can be stressful because of the expectations aroused in adults, and feeling the odd-one-out amongst other children.

Many young people consider that the educational system is inappropriate as a preparation for life. Feeling this, while yet having to conform to school norms, is one of the factors in teenage stress.

In adolescence, the child still has little experience of life and how to cope with it. He yearns for personal and financial independence, yet is still partly or wholly dependent on his parents. Also, the adolescent wants emotional and intellectual independence from his parents but is still tied in many overt and subtle ways. It is a time of swings between wanting to be an adult and free, and wanting to be a child and protected, a time of critically challenging parental values. The stress on the parents is of having to re-examine their values in the face of sometimes very unsubtle criticism.

It is natural for parents to feel a certain envy for their teenagers' freedom, youth, and seemingly easy life – for all the unsureness and self-doubts of that age group. This should not become a source of stress for either the parents or the children. The question of privacy, both physical and psychological, has to be resolved, too.

It is only the overly-sheltered or the very tough-minded who seem to sail through adolescence without stress. The physical changes of maturation also have to be coped with. Relationships, particularly sexual and emotional ones with other adolescents, are often tentative or unstable, and can be a particular source of stress. There may be doubts over sexual orientation or misgivings over sexual attractiveness; whether or not to become sexually active preoccupies many teenagers.

Teenagers' problems and anxieties can show themselves in behavioural disturbances such as hooliganism, gang-fights, truancy. It is not uncommon for children in their early teens to go on shop-lifting expeditions and to risk brushes with the law for pilfering and mindless vandalism. This may be revolt, or a reaction to boredom, on the part of the children. The parents have to find a middle way between apparent apathy and open anger or shock, and should show that they care, without actively interfering. What they should try not to do is relieve their own stresses at the expense of their children.

when old

The middle age of life (which in women includes the menopause) is classically regarded as a time of stress. Having to worry about elderly parents, particularly when they start to be ailing and failing, takes over from worrying about the children.

Reappraising one's life at mid-point can show up the missed opportunities, with the realisation that what has not yet been achieved, may never be.

The so-called 'mid-life crisis' is a period of readjustment; some people cope less well than others with the stresses that occur. But by middle age, many people have at least learned what they like and do not like, so there is a better chance of following one's true inclinations and of building up interests outside work or the immediate family. This may also help towards a less stressful old age. Loneliness can be a grave stress – at any age. It is easier to make friends by following some interest which can be shared, rather than trying to seek out people merely for the sake of combating loneliness.

The stresses of old age can be made worse by lack of resources and reserves. Some old people who are now retired feel useless, particularly someone who is now living under more straitened circumstances. Worse, he (or more usually she) may have lost a spouse.

Physical illness in old age is a further source of stress, particularly chronic or crippling disease and handicaps. Being housebound can aggravate the situation, and so can awareness of failing mental and physical powers, and the worry about 'being a burden'. The sense of futility and uselessness may depress and stress an old person to the point of contemplating suicide – even after a full life well spent. Being made to feel useful and needed can be as important as proper physical care in old age.

Stress may be mitigated by the old person's long experience of life: he has seen it all before, and has developed strategies for dealing with untoward or unusual occurrences. However, some old people lose their adaptability and their resourcefulness, and personality characteristics become exaggerated, the old person becoming more suspicious, or more irritable or more difficult; the younger ones can help by reassurance – and much patience.

◗ **National Council for Carers and their Elderly Dependants,** 29 Chilworth Mews, London w2 3RG (telephone 01-262 1451) provides a service of information and guidance for people who have or have had the care of elderly or infirm dependants at home. There are local branches which provide fellowship and watch over the interests of carers with dependants.

Stress in marriage

Marriage requires a series of adaptations by the partners in order to establish a close, intimate and committed partnership, after being a protected member inside a family, or being single, with perhaps only oneself to please.

And when the first baby is born, there has to be further adaptation from twosome to threesome, and moresome for second and third children. Then there are changing parental roles when these children start school, then leave school; and when 'the nest is emptied' there has to be adaptation back to a twosome. Then more adaptation in retirement and old age, and finally to loss of partner and widowhood.

Change and the threat of change invariably causes some degree of stress; new and demanding circumstances raise the level of anxiety. A strong, supportive relationship makes the uncertainties tolerable, and helps people through periods of adjustment. In the past, when marriages were more difficult to dissolve, the legal and domestic framework supported the partners while they made these adjustments, with varying degrees of ease or success.

Even an unstable marriage provides a domestic framework: the breakfast needs making even if the row of the previous evening has left a chilled atmosphere. The framework which a stable relationship provides can support people when they are faced with critical events in their lives, such as prolonged illness, death of a parent or child, or change in employment or geographical location. In 1982, unemployment, or its threat, can be added to the list of unwanted changes forced on people.

To an increasing degree, marriage is under pressure to meet high expectations and to live up to the ideals of romantic love in a social climate in which people have great freedom of choice about how they conduct their lives, and the amount of togetherness or separateness they maintain.

The emphasis on the individual and on the rights of the individual in marriage, as in other areas of life, can, when overstated, be in conflict with the idea of committed partnership and responsibility.

the roles

Of the many social changes affecting marriage, one of the most influential is the breakdown of clear and differentiated roles between men and women. Until fairly recently, the traditional roles of the man and the woman in the marriage were well-defined. Put simply, the man went out to work, the woman looked after the home and had children. By and large, this state of affairs was fairly general until the second world war. Since then, an increasing proportion of women are going out to work, usually before and after bringing up their children. The woman's continuing wage-earning means that she is not financially dependent on the man. The man who is made aware of his apparent redundancy may be stressed by this.

The breakdown of traditional roles with the apparent, but in some respects illusory, emancipation of women can lead to stress in both partners. The woman may feel trapped by her biological role and feel that she is not fulfilling her potential as a mother if she does not have children, or her potential in the work place when she does have them.

One cause of stress in marriage today is the envy, often unconscious, of the opposite sex; women envy the still greater opportunities open to men in their careers; men envy the fact that it is still only the women who can bear the children.

Work interests may clash: the man may expect his wife to subordinate her career prospects to his, or his frequent changes of location may disrupt her career. Her resentment can produce marital friction and stress. Where a woman outshines the husband professionally, he may feel threatened and be under stress and the marriage suffers.

conflict

Emotions operate intensely in marriage, as they do in any close relationship and, inevitably, lead to some measure of conflict, frustration and aggressive reaction against the partner. A measure of aggression and hate is inevitable in all love relationships; the opposite would be indifference.

There will inevitably be conflict of feeling when experience does not match expectations (realistic or otherwise) and when the expectations of one partner do not resemble those of the other. For many people, marriage is initially very idealised, invested with hope for what has not been realised before. This is particularly so for people who marry because of an inability to manage a life on their own, or who use marriage as an escape-hatch from an unhappy home with their parents.

choice of partner

People seem to choose their partners for unconscious, as well as conscious, reasons in an attempt to resolve old conflicts. Some people look for a marriage partner who will complement them so that their 'other half' can be and can do what they cannot be or do themselves. This can work well provided that the difference is appreciated rather than resented. Taken to excess, it can lead to grim conflict.

Other marriages are based on identification, a wish for alikeness, even a submission to the other personality. Stress is caused when it is reluctantly discovered that the partner is a separate and different person who sometimes reacts opposingly to the same event.

People are usually at their most critical when the faults in their partner reflect something in themselves which they cannot handle and do not wish to know about. There is no such thing, outside the realm of imagination, as a marriage free from conflict. If conflict and the stress that derives from it can be seen in a positive light, they can provide the impetus to change and to becoming more mature.

having children

With the availability of effective contraception, women can decide not to have children. Children cause stress as well as delight. Childless couples may seem to get more companionship out of their marriage, and many people with children say that their marital satisfaction was highest before they had children.

Freedom to make the decision is not, however, necessarily comfortable:

the responsibility is in itself a cause of stress. The process of choosing can arouse conflict within and between partners. The decision whether or not to have children is rarely made on a wholly rational basis.

The birth of a first child may predominantly mean delight for one person, a source of anxiety for another. For most people, it will mean both things and there will be conflicting feelings.

The needs of children and the demands of careers can be in prolonged conflict. A woman at work during the day is apt to feel resentful that she still has to do the housework, cook and put the children to bed. Too few men share the domestic chores to any appreciable extent, clinging on to their traditional role.

While there is joy in a first baby, there is also loss of freedom, for some women the temporary or permanent loss of a job or a career; for both husband and wife, the loss of neat pairing. People appear to make better adjustments to new situations when they can recognise and mourn what they have had to give up. Only then, it seems, can they fully appreciate the satisfactions of the altered circumstances.

◗ **Exploring Parenthood,** 54 Parkhill Road, London NW3 2YP (telephone 01-485 0299) offers a partnership between parents and experts in the fields of child, adolescent and family development, in the belief that looking at issues beforehand can help avoid family stress and break-down. Activities include support groups and workshops.

sex

Marital uneasiness can be made worse by specific incompatibilities. Sexual difficulties are a common source of stress. Frequency and type of sexual intercourse should be by mutual consent but this may be difficult to attain. One partner may impose his or her wish for more or less frequent intercourse or may demand practices distasteful to the partner. Where such lack of mutual adjustment remains an unspoken problem, it can constitute a nagging stress. Over-emphasis on the sexual aspects of marriage or unreal expectations in one or other partner can lead to unnecessary dissatisfaction and stress. Becoming aware of one's own true reactions and being able to talk to the partner about sexual problems may be the first step towards solving them.

Where stress leads to impotence or premature ejaculation in the man or frigidity in the woman and reluctance to have sex, this can lead to further tension within the relationship. Help is available for persistent problems and should be sought before matters become serious.

There are sexual dysfunction clinics or psychosexual clinics in several large hospitals and in some marriage guidance centres, and in some family planning clinics within the NHS. Some general practitioners offer psychosexual counselling.

Marital infidelities are a well-known stress in marriage, and they may reflect the stresses existing in the marriage as well as causing new ones. Sometimes an extra-marital affair of which evidence is left lying about can be a symptom of dissatisfaction and an unspoken request for the partner to help in doing something about the lack of growth or the stultification of the relationship. The stress it causes may lead to a permanent separation or, when the shock has worn off, it may open the way to a more satisfactory marriage.

quarrelling

'A quarrel a day keeps divorce away' may not be everybody's ideal of marital satisfaction, but arguments and even quarrels are not necessarily destructive if the dissatisfaction, frustration, conflicts, even fury, can be expressed in words and people are willing to listen to each other.

If the argument, although heated, is always related to trivialities or a particular triviality, this usually means that the quarrel is really about something more fundamental and help may be needed to understand the underlying meaning. Try to analyse your last quarrel: was your anger directed at the right person (difficulties at work taken out on husband?); were you arguing about the right thing (ostensibly about the washing up, but perhaps really about who neglected whom over the past few weeks?); was the timing an aggravating factor (when the in-laws were coming to visit?); did it reveal past grievances that you thought long dead and forgotten (harbouring grudges can only lead to stress).

However distressing arguments and quarrels may be, they at least release tension. Continuously repressed feelings which fester can cause extreme tiredness and give rise to physical and psychiatric symptoms.

dealing with conflict

The first step in resolving any conflict is to decide what the conflict is really about. Often, a surface issue is only a symbol of an underlying more crucial conflict. Thus, not being able to decide with your spouse where to go for a holiday, although a minor problem in itself, may reflect a conflict over who makes major decisions and how.

If you keep on having disagreements about the same sort of thing, identifying the recurring theme may reveal the real conflict associated with it. If hostility continues despite seemingly solving the apparent conflict, deeper issues will need to be brought into the open and resolved.

Learning to identify the causes of conflict requires practice. The types of issue that often lie at the bottom of conflicts are conflict

– over roles (for example, if a wife wants a husband to share in the domestic chores but he thinks this violates his concept of masculinity)

– over values (for example, following an altruistic but ill-paid career as against a lucrative but socially dubious one)

– over spending and saving

– over who gets their way (for instance, if one person always chooses the tv programme despite the protests of the rest of the family)

– over being right on factual matters (some people are both opinionated and reluctant to put their facts to the test).

Being over-assertive can also give rise to conflict. Standing up for one's rights may be useful when dealing with bureaucratic bumbledom but is a recipe for disaster in family discussion. Winning a point may alienate the rest of the family; it may be better to concede one point in order to set up favourable conditions for the resolution of other conflicts. The art of compromise needs to be learnt by many people who take into marital and family life the uncompromising attitudes and stances which they believe necessary at work.

When a set of working rules and agreements has to be arrived at in the family, it is better to spell them out; it can lead to stress if members of the family arrive at different rules under the mistaken impression that a consensus has been agreed.

seeking help

The ease of divorce has led to a destabilisation of marriage, to a growing feeling that a marriage is not necessarily 'for keeps'. Although divorce is relatively simple, and repairing a marriage is difficult, it is important that a couple who take the initial vows seriously and have a marital problem, seek help sooner rather than later – before bitterness and hurt drive them further and further apart.

❍ The headquarters of various marriage guidance or advisory councils are **National Marriage Guidance Council,** Herbert Gray College, Little Church Street, Rugby CV21 3AP (telephone 0788-73241); **Scottish Marriage Guidance Council,** 26 Frederick Street, Edinburgh EH2 2JR (telephone 031-225 5006); **Catholic Marriage Advisory Council,** 15 Lansdowne Road, London W11 3AJ (telephone 01-727 0141); **Jewish Marriage Council,** 4a Somerset Road, off Ravenshurst Avenue, London NW4 4EJ (telephone 01-203 6311).

Interviews are by appointment, mostly made by telephone, or by personal application to the larger offices. A first appointment might be offered within a few days, but in some places it may be a few weeks. Interviews last up to an hour; they are generally weekly.

A counsellor is trained to help people to talk about their marital problems in order to see their difficulties in a clearer perspective and to consider the possible courses of action open to them. Counselling may therefore be a lengthy process, taking several interviews. The councils have psychiatric consultants, with whom counsellors work closely. Application to a marriage guidance council can be made jointly by a couple or individually by either husband or wife. Counselling can be successful without the other spouse attending as well.

For many people it is not easy to approach a counselling body: it seems an admission of failure and unhappiness.

Inherent in the process of seeking help is the wish for change, but the change needs to be in oneself as well as in the partner. Counselling that is used as a forum for blame will prove ineffective. The prospect of change in oneself, however, is frightening and in itself raises anxiety: change is a step into the unknown, and its outcome cannot be predicted.

The work with a marriage guidance counsellor – and it can be hard work – may lead to a more satisfying marriage. Or it may lead to a positive or less destructive separation. Today, the aim of marriage counselling is not to save marriages at all costs; there is more concern about emotional growth and development of insight so that even if a marriage has to end, the same type of mistake need not be made a second time.

◖ For those who find it difficult to seek help in their own locality, the **Institute of Marital Studies,** Tavistock Centre, 120 Belsize Lane, London NW3 5BA (telephone 01-435 7111), a centre of advanced study and practice in marital work, offers a therapeutic service. Both partners must attend for regular weekly interviews. Fees are assessed according to financial circumstances and can be waived if income is limited to state benefit. Further information from the appointments secretary.

When people are faced with uncertainty all around, they need something of their own which feels safe and sane, and which will hold them in other areas of their lives. A 'confiding relationship' is important in managing emotional stress. For many people, marriage is the most significant of confiding relationships.

Marriage has never been more open to question, and yet more people are married than ever before, many people divorce in order to marry again, and the expectations placed on marriage appear to remain as strong as ever – and so does the need for affection, humour, loyalty, kindness, tolerance, support.

Stress in divorce

Marriage is more difficult to get out of than to get into, not only legally and materially, but also emotionally. A divorce (other than that which legalises a long-standing separation) is never free from stress, tension, conflict, regret, apprehension, sadness and pain.

During the long drawn-out process of disengagement, the participants fluctuate between hope and despair before one or both partners finally will acknowledge that their marriage is a failure, for which it is no longer worthwhile to make the sacrifice and effort required to maintain it. Separation, even when it is not felt as a supreme tragedy, presents a difficult period of transition from one type of life to another, with all its uncertainties which may continue for many years beyond the decree nisi.

There are obvious differences in the impact on the partner who finds him/herself unloved, rejected, imposed on or only reluctantly agreeing to the divorce and the one who is the prime mover, accepts the responsibility, does the leaving. However, the situation is rarely so unambiguous: the rejected sometimes becomes the rejector, the 'innocent' is beset with guilt. Both partners are likely to feel aggrieved, misused, condemned by the other. The lives of both undergo disruption with regard to children, family, friends; and both have to negotiate a change of social identity.

In terms of stress, divorce ranks second only to bereavement in the list of factors; some people who have experienced both say that being divorced is more desolating than being widowed. Widowhood usually invites an unambiguous sympathy and a degree of support not generally afforded to the divorced; the elements of choice and responsibility, shame, a sense of failure or humiliation, and even of condemnation do not figure in widowhood.

In both situations there is loss. In the divorce, there is loss of a particular lifestyle, perhaps loss of home; maybe loss of sexual intimacy, bodily contact and warmth; for one partner, loss of day-to-day contact with children; and, perhaps most distressing of all, loss of hope and ideals. There is, therefore, much to be mourned, however difficult the preceding circumstances may have been.

mourning

In any normal mourning process there are certain discernible phases which may overlap. After the first shock and disbelief that 'this could happen to me', there is a phase of acute anxiety and disorientation when the implications of the loss start to make themselves felt. Then, during a phase of yearning and searching for what is lost, many desperate 'last attempts' at reconciliation may be made, despite the realisation of a 'lost cause'. This is followed by a phase of anger, uncomfortably mixed with guilt. Finally, there is a period of emptiness, before hope renews itself and the person can find new meaning in life. The whole process may well take two years after a bereavement. After a divorce it may take five.

Mourning ceases to be normal when the process is unduly prolonged or stuck in one phase or another; for example, if anger gets more and more vitriolic, or the search for what is lost becomes waiting for a miraculous return.

Loss of identity is a very basic fear, so is the fear of being found unlovable and of being destructive. At separation, these fears contribute to the panic and sense of isolation, and may even impair judgment. When the fundamental fear of abandonment threatens, an adult can be paralysed with feelings of helplessness and insecurity, particularly someone who has had an insecure childhood.

There is often an amazing sense of continuing attachment and belonging, either to the person one wants to leave or to the person who has left, even when love has died. For some people it seems remarkably tenacious and, even after many years of separation, dormant feelings of attachment to an ex-spouse can be reawakened. This sense of connectedness may prevent people from going through the necessary mourning for what has been lost, and makes it difficult for the abandoned partner not to construe any kind word or considerate action on the part of the deserter as a gesture of reconciliation. Even the abandoner, going directly to another potentially permanent mate, may, instead of finding relief, be unable to shake off feelings of extreme disequilibrium.

mixed feelings

Most people have mixed feelings about divorce and continue to wonder whether they should try harder. But if something is inevitable, it does not help to put it off for too long.

Some people deal with uncertainty by denying its existence and cutting the knot as swiftly and as cleanly as possible, in an urge to get it all over and done with. The speed with which divorces can be obtained is not always helpful: people can find themselves taken over by a legal process which outstrips their emotional capacities while they remain hopelessly entangled and divided in their feelings. Some solicitors are attuned to the ambivalence, and recognise the signs when the initial request for legal advice is to be used only as a threat to the marriage partner. They may help by referring the couple to a counselling agency; others are not so perceptive.

The primitive feelings of anger and hurt are sometimes then re-directed on to the problems of apportionment of money and property and prolonged disputes over care of and access to children. The problems are real enough and there may be no 'right' answer, but some couples find it difficult to achieve any form of agreement and are unable seriously to consider what would be best for the children, because in their bruised and insecure state, they feel more childlike than adult themselves. Sometimes the fight is unconsciously maintained to ward off the grief and emptiness that might follow: a fight is one way of prolonging a relationship.

the children

When and how to tell the children is a problem for most people, particularly when they have tried to hide the conflict and have not wanted to disturb the children unnecessarily before a firm decision is made. However, children have long antennae and long ears, even when doors are closed, and are uncannily perceptive to atmosphere. Leaving them in the dark when their every sense tells them that their world is about to fall apart, can cause them even greater stress.

The children will inevitably be upset in their own right, suffering their own separation anxiety, and perhaps showing symptoms of quite severe disturbance. Bad behaviour hides an anxiety about what is going to happen to them in the threatened separation which they may fear is all their fault. It is a tremendous burden for children to carry their parents' marriage if they know that they are the only reason for its maintenance, but most children initially try to get their parents to stay together.

Less stressful for the adults are children who develop a precocious maturity, act as conciliators, and end up by parenting their parents. Some bad behaviour is a much healthier reaction: children who are forced into a false maturity are later likely to show the distress they suffered when the situation is again safe enough for them to do so.

Children can be seriously affected by continued parental conflict in the home. They are also upset and disturbed by their parents' separating and by sometimes radically changed circumstances in their lives. Their school work is likely to deteriorate because they will be less able to concentrate while they are worrying about what is going to happen to them and until they are assured in fact, as well as in words, that they have not lost their parents' love and concern and that they do not miss out too much under the new arrangements. During this period they may be more vulnerable to infections and accidents, and they may become more babyish in their behaviour. All of this is very stressful to an already distressed parent.

Children are, however, adaptable creatures and, as their worlds settle down again, they can recover their equilibrium. There may be aspects they dislike and some features which cause stress; for some time they may be very angry with the missing parent; but some may recover more quickly than the parents.

Adults (and their children) cannot avoid the problems and stress inherent in divorce, and it is difficult to prepare people in advance for something they hope will not happen to them. While the NHS provides antenatal classes, and the local authority runs pre-retirement courses, there is no formal preparation for divorce or separation. People can, however, attempt to learn from the experience of those around them in similar circumstances. They will find support when they discover that their fears and feelings are not abnormal and that others have felt likewise. If mourning can be allowed to run its course, and feelings of loss, anger and guilt are allowed to surface, they help in the healing process. Thwarted and stored up, these emotions may cause breakdown later if a second severe loss is experienced. When there is something to grieve for, grief is healthy.

professional help

People should not be too afraid, if necessary, to seek professional help: friends and relatives may not allow them to show their grief or let them reiterate the whys and wherefores of the breakdown of the marriage. Professional ears are used to such anguish, know what is within the realm of the normal and can lend emotional strength. An hour a week with a psychotherapist, marriage guidance counsellor or social worker dealing jointly with the disturbed feelings may enable a distressed person to get through the rest of the week.

Many more marital problems are taken to general practitioners than to the specialist agencies; sometimes the problem is presented directly and openly, sometimes through an illness. Some GPs are prepared to listen and even offer a follow-up; most can provide an appropriate referral.

Marriage guidance agencies offer their services to those who want help in parting (not only to those who want help to stay together) and to those who, caught up in the ambivalence, just do not know what they want.

There are also some new conciliation services in various parts of the country, some independent and voluntary (sometimes fee-charging), some attached directly to the courts as units of the probation and after-care service. These services are designed to help couples who have made the decision to divorce but are unable to come to an agreement on their own regarding the care of the children and apportionment of resources. They aim to help people to separate as constructively as possible. Citizens' advice bureaux should be able to provide addresses and details.

Anyone who thinks divorce is easy should not contemplate it.

◑ **Gingerbread,** 35 Wellington Street, London WC2 (telephone 01-240 0953) is a nationwide organisation providing support for single parents and their children. There are self-help groups throughout the country, organising such services as baby sitting, crisis support, playschool schemes, holiday schemes (telephone numbers obtainable by ringing national office). There is a phone-in advice service.

◑ **National Council for the Divorced and Separated,** 13 High Street, Little Shelford, Cambridge, CB2 5ES, has over 100 branches throughout the British Isles which provide a venue where people with similar experiences and problems can meet and make new friends and develop new interests. Most branches have a welfare officer; there is also an individual member scheme.

◑ **The National Council for One Parent Families,** 255 Kentish Town Road, London NW5 2LX (telephone 01-267 1361) offers help and advice. The service is free and confidential and includes legal advice and help with problems such as housing, social security, taxation and maintenance.

If you live in a London borough south of the Thames, contact **One Parent Families,** South London Advice Centre, 20 Clapham Common South Side, London SW4 7AB (telephone 01-720 9191).

◑ **National Federation of Solo Clubs for widowed, divorced, separated and single people,** 7/8 Ruskin Chambers, 191 Corporation Street, Birmingham 4 (telephone 021-236-2879) has affiliated clubs throughout the country which organise varied activities and also holidays at home and abroad. Each club has a welfare officer.

◑ **National Family Conciliation Council,** Hon. Sec. Mr Ken Leuillette, 'Llanberis', Brooklands Way, East Grinstead, West Sussex, is a co-ordinating body for independent out-of-court conciliation services whose aim is to bring parents together to discuss their future plans and the implications for their children, particularly custody and access. There are at present 20 affiliated services.

Stress in work

As most people spend a third of their waking life at work, problems or incompatibilities there can provide a major stress.

The stresses may involve the work itself – from phrenetic or repetitive tasks on the assembly line to the lonely boredom of a night-watchman. A meticulous person may find it stressful to work on an assembly line at a set pace which does not give him the opportunity to check the quality of the work. By contrast, a brilliant improvisor may be irked by having to do things by the book.

Research on the stressful effects of mass-production techniques has shown that stress is decreased when work is done in small groups.

When work groups are too large, relationships between some individuals become attenuated and the group loses cohesion. It may split up into sub-groups which become cliques or even cabals. Friction between the leaders of groups, reflecting their ambitions and mutual jealousies, may be reflected in the withholding of cooperation by the members of one group towards another. In big organisations, people sometimes fear other departments more than their competitors.

The stress that machines produce is generally predictable; that produced by people is often unpredictable. Conflicts with other people at work can engender a great deal of stress. Most people have very little say in the choice of their workmates. A pool of secretaries may be disrupted and stressed by a fussy or a slovenly/lazy newcomer. In dangerous jobs, lack of full trust in a workmate is particularly stressful because a lapse on his part may endanger others.

Problems with employers are notoriously stressful. The employer has important powers over his employees even though these powers are governed or curtailed by legislation about security of employment and by union rules. (But a resourceful employer can sometimes make conditions at work so stressful for an employee he wishes to get rid of that the employee leaves of his or her own accord.) The employee is in an ambivalent relationship with his employer: on the one hand he is indebted to the employer for his livelihood (particularly during periods of high unemployment), on the other, he may have grievances about his salary, promotion prospects, status, perks, lack of consideration and so on. Some psychoanalysts consider that this reflects, in a minor degree, the ambivalent relationship between a young person and the authoritarian figure of his father, and that people who have not developed a workable relationship with earlier authority figures, such as parents and teachers, may have difficulties with their employers.

Even a sympathetic employer or personnel officer may not appreciate how stressful a job or part of a job can be. But analysing it into its elements might identify which component of the job contributes most to the stress. Quite small modifications may help, either singly or, more likely, when added together. If physical conditions are adverse, resorting to one of the many regulations governing working conditions may improve the work environment and lessen stress.

A change in attitude may be needed rather than any change in the nature of the work itself, or its environment. Ask yourself realistically what part it plays in your life. Is it a 9 to 5 routine which pays the bills? If so, stripping it down to its essentials may lessen stressful aspects. If your work is the centre point of your life, you should carefully consider all its aspects as they affect you, your ideals and expectations, and even ask yourself whether you should think in terms of changing your job.

A salutary exercise, if your job is unsatisfying and your work seems full of stress, might be to imagine how you would feel if tomorrow you were told that you have to stop being in the job (perhaps being made redundant). Such a thought might help to put some of the difficulties into perspective.

Work is not only important for obvious economic reasons but, for many people, bound up with a deeply engrained work ethic and a way of proving themselves. When there is pressure on people to better themselves, to stay on at school, go to college or university, attend day release or evening classes, they then expect to be promoted in line with their skills, qualifications and experience. They resent it if they are not, particularly if they feel that promotion is being unjustifiably withheld. The stress of feeling overlooked is then followed by the stress of wondering whether the failure to achieve promotion might indeed reflect personal inadequacies.

overwork or absenteeism

Overwork not only causes stress but may itself be a symptom of stress, either arising from work itself or reflecting problems at home or in the family. For instance strained relationships, particularly marital ones, can lead to an escape into (over)work.

Overwork manifests itself as long hours, not always productive, hurried meal breaks, taking work home (if the work is of that type), and reluctance to take short breaks or longer holidays, which sets up a vicious circle of stress. A person may find himself unable to cope with his work, either because of intrinsic inadequacies, or because new technologies are making increasing demands on him, or because he has been promoted beyond his level of competence. People can be promoted too rapidly and too far. The 'Peter principle' states that in a hierarchy every employee tends to rise to his level of incompetence, that is, being promoted away from a job he can accomplish, to one just outside his competence. At that level, whether the incompetence is appreciated by the person or not, stress results because the job is now in essence impossible. Overwork and frustration lead to a build up of major stress and sometimes even severe physical illness such as a heart attack.

For some people, even when the goals have been reached, it may be difficult to ease up. Years of striving for promotion and recognition have become a way of life, and a deliberate effort has to be made to lessen the pressures.

Some people react to stress not by overwork but by the opposite, absenteeism. This is especially likely if the work is arduous, too difficult, or plain boring, as so many routine jobs are. Some people never adapt to their jobs, always finding them a chore, distasteful, tedious or unrewarding. Lessening the stress by taking odd days off is only a very short-term solution.

Employers, on the other hand, see things their way and may feel stressed by what to them seems indolence, unreliability or sheer dishonesty on the part of their employees. They may regard employment legislation as molly-coddling and the unions as self-interest groups who take a blinkered attitude to the long-term prospects of the company.

Where the real employer is a statutory body, nameless, faceless and unapproachable to the average employee, and the apparent employer is merely an agent, for example for the local authority or the health service, he has responsibility for the employee without real power. If problems arise, both find the situation stressful; but there are arbitration and appeal procedures which, even though elaborate or in some cases inadequate, may help to defuse such situations.

special stresses

Shift work incorporates stresses of a particular kind. The body has very definite, built-in, daily rhythms. For example, the secretion of the hormone cortisol (hydrocortisone) which protects against stress effects, is lowest during sleep. With shift work (as in jet-lag), these rhythms are disrupted and the shift-worker has bodily stresses added to any psychological ones. People who are on permanent or long term night shifts are much less stressed than those who work a cycle of 2 or 3 different shifts every few weeks. However, the unsociable hours associated with permanent early, late or night shifts can also constitute a stress.

Some jobs involve contact and even conflict with people who are themselves stressed. For example, traffic wardens encounter harrassed motorists looking for somewhere to park, bus conductors have to face long queues of angry commuters; a doctor is expected to reassure an anxious sick person, a social worker to deal with a family under stress. Do not add to their stress: it is not fair to take it out on people who are only doing their job.

redundancy and unemployment

Unemployment affects not only the unemployed themselves, but also their families and, if it is sufficiently widespread, the community in which they live. There is also a link between unemployment and ill health and between unemployment and earlier death, including death from heart disease. There is also a correlation between unemployment and higher rates of admission to mental hospitals and prisons, more deaths, suicides and murders.

Generally, prolonged unemployment means a significant decline in standard of living – which leads to stress related to the obvious economic problems.

But the stress is due not only to loss of income but to the loss of shared experiences and contact with people outside the home and to the loss of identity associated with one's job. This can quickly turn to a feeling of futility, and a lack of confidence about one's ability to get a job or to hold one down if offered. If, after a while, the unemployed person loses heart, he may become poorly motivated to seek work. Marital friction may develop or increase through being cooped up all day or if the wife becomes the only breadwinner.

There are stages in people's psychological reaction to unemployment: at first shock and disbelief, but tempered with a certain optimism and sense of being on holiday. This gives way to a sense of meaningless leisure, inertia and exhaustion, with a loss of self-esteem, anxiety and depression, and tensions in the family; lastly comes a chronic state of passive acceptance marked by submissiveness, a feeling of inferiority, a lack of identity, a restricted way of life and little hope of change.

Almost as bad as unemployment is the fear of redundancy. Uncertainty can cause as much stress as a definite setback. But redundancy or dismissal do not usually occur without any warning. People who are in danger of losing their job should begin to work out a strategy for survival: from sorting out financial affairs to planning how to occupy their time.

Unemployment increases stress because it disturbs daily patterns. It is wise to get up at the same time as when going to work, or at some other, reasonable, fixed time; meals should be at regular times. It may be possible to find some part-time work or earn money at home by using a skill. If no money-earning activities seem available, it could be a good idea to use the time to develop a useful skill (such as typing, cooking) which might be put to profitable use later.

People often complain that they do not have the time to do things they would like. The enforced leisure of unemployment could well be used to do some of these things though, surprisingly, it will require considerable self-discipline.

Finding some form of voluntary work will give a sense of usefulness and the satisfaction of being with others: helping with children or old people, giving help in a hospital, especially if there is a league of friends; helping to teach someone to read. Local libraries and the local social services departments usually have details of organisations needing help.

People interested in voluntary work should contact their local volunteer bureau or council for voluntary service (or, in country areas, community council or council of community service). These will be listed in Yellow Pages under *social service and welfare organisations*. Details of volunteer bureaux or of councils for voluntary service or of community councils can be obtained from

◑ **National Council for Voluntary Organisations,** 26 Bedford Square, London WC1B 3HU (telephone 01-636 4066) or from

◑ **Volunteer Centre,** 29 Lower Kings Road, Berkhamsted, Herts HP4 2AB (telephone 04427-73311).

Many people need help in one way or another: water your neighbours' garden while they are on holiday or if they are too disabled to do so themselves, walk their dog, push their wheelchair, cut their hedge, shave him or give her a manicure. There is a lot to be done if you use your imagination and initiative; look around you and ask "who is my neighbour?".

It is also important to keep as fit as possible while unemployed. This should be easy as there is more time for exercise or sport. But paradoxically a great deal of discipline is necessary (it helps to set aside a regular time). Exercise has the extra advantage of being a good antidote for stress.

The world around us

Big cities can be very unfriendly places for people, particularly young ones who drift into them, seeking work or adventure. Financial pressures may lead to a person taking an ill-paid job without prospects or drifting into petty crime. Crime and vandalism are a major source of stress. Where elderly people are afraid to leave their home unaccompanied because of the risk of being robbed or mugged, a neighbour's help is not just a personal good deed but can help towards community spirit.

Burglary is also increasing and being burgled is an especial stress. At least taking the commonsense precautions of having good locks and using them may deter the casual opportunist burglar (maybe a teenager on the loose), and avoid unnecessary stress.

noise

Noise is a major source of stress. We are assailed by noise on all sides. Inescapable noise such as traffic noise close to trunk roads and motorways often reaches intolerable levels and so does aircraft noise for people living under the approach flight path of busy airports; there is also the relentlessness of pop music in shops and pubs – those, however, you can avoid.

Be aware that you too may be adding to somebody else's stress by banging car doors, keeping the engine running in the early hours of the night, or a non-suppressed motorbike. Often the person who unwittingly creates noise (with typewriter, vacuum cleaner, electric drill) that is intolerable to others, is less aware of it, and less affected by it, than the people around. If possible, use noisy equipment only when there is no one else around, so as not to push up the general stress levels.

crowding

The sheer number of human beings milling about, queueing up for things, obstructing each other, is a stress for city dwellers. Overcrowding is a known source of stress which has been studied in laboratory animals. A colony of mice will increase in number rapidly, but when a peak is reached it is not maintained and the mouse population actually decreases despite the space being the same and food being freely available. In human societies, population densities above a certain value are inherently stressful too, but humans being less sensible than mice, overcrowding continues and increases in cities. In overcrowded and under-privileged areas there is competition for space, amenities and facilities. The stresses may be partly offset where the pressures have the effect of generating community mutual aid.

The mushrooming of cities has led to severe transport problems. Buses or taxis, where available, become hopelessly bogged down in traffic jams; the commuter is forced to use his car and the increase in private cars adds to the traffic jams.

It is commonplace in big cities for commuters to drive for an hour or more in the morning and evening rush-hours. Driving in heavy traffic has been shown to be a powerful stress, with rapid and extreme rises in heart rate and blood pressure.

driving

Driving can be stressful even for people who are not subject to stress in other areas of their lives. (As against this, some people find that going for a drive can help them to unwind when they are tense or angry.)

The stress in driving comes from the accumulation of factors – traffic, weather conditions, getting lost, trouble with the car, noise and vibration, passengers, fatigue.

Fatigue in driving is partly due to prolonged muscular contraction, caused by sitting in an incorrect posture, or by tension from anxiety. While muscles are contracted, their blood vessels are compressed and this reduces their supply of oxygen and nutrients and slows down the removal of waste products from the muscle cells. Muscle fatigue gets worse and worse if the person remains in the same position.

Stress can be caused by the passengers, particularly children. Passengers should not nag, and should aim to make the driver's task as easy as possible; children should be taught from the start never to distract the driver. They are less likely to do this if they sit in the back and are given games and activities. If they do create a disturbance, or get noisy, the driver should stop the car as soon as possible, explaining that it is not safe to drive in those conditions.

The act of driving itself can have a profound effect on people. Not only do aggressive people become more so, but people who are normally civilised and restrained may suddenly reveal a savage side. Being inside the car, shut off from other people, acts as a form of insulation and this gives people a sense of security and makes aggression safer because there is no face to face confrontation. Also, it is easy to impute hostile and negative feelings to the other driver: people can work up quite a hate feeling for the driver in the car behind or in front of them, take it as a personal insult if someone overtakes them (especially in a more powerful car, or a woman driver) and then try to make it hard for the driver concerned. Such retaliation not only causes extra stress but is dangerous.

There will always be aggressive, antisocial, indecisive drivers (and drivers who are just plain incompetent) and it is no use trying to get back at them. Drive your own car carefully, calmly, competently and courteously, and hope that the other people will do likewise. Remember that it is better to arrive safely than to travel in a rage.

Becoming impatient and irritated by the traffic will make you feel stressed (and upset your passengers) and will not get you to your destination more quickly – it is also likely to cause you to make mistakes.

Make sure you are comfortable behind the wheel; check that your shoulders are not contracted and hunched, that your neck is not jutting forward, your teeth not clenched and your hands holding but not tightly gripping the wheel.

Relax the shoulder muscles, take care that your back is well supported, relax your jaw and face muscles. When held up at a traffic light, relieve neck tension by small circling movements of your head, or try to practise slow breathing and tell yourself to relax as you breathe out.

It is helpful if you can find time to relax before you begin a long drive, even just a few minutes are better than nothing. Obviously it is best to set out fresh, having had adequate sleep the night before, and to be neither hungry nor too replete.

You should try not to drive for more than 3 hours without a break. An overtired driver gets more and more uncomfortable and starts to lose concentration. It is important to allow for regular brief stops, some of which could include eating something (a biscuit will do) and a precautionary pee. If you stop at a lay-by or service area, go for a short walk to exercise the muscles and stimulate blood circulation, or even have a short nap. A tired driver is a danger to himself and to other road users.

Be particularly careful when driving home at the end of a long and tiring day, slow down a little if you normally tend to be a fast driver. Sometimes when everybody else, motorists, cyclists and pedestrians, seem to be getting in the way or doing stupid things, it is worth asking yourself: 'Is it them or me?'.

accidents

Some accident-prone people appear always to be having accidents of one kind or another – on the road, in the home, at work. Some accidents are genuinely fortuitous, others are due to stupidity or bravado or lack of foresight.

Stress can predispose towards accidents in several ways: by making the person more preoccupied and forgetful, failing to carry out routine safety procedures. Someone worrying about problems at home or at work is not giving his full attention to what he is doing or to his immediate surroundings. Stress and anxiety may be associated with incoordination of movements, shakiness and clumsiness.

A stressed person may have an unconscious wish to express his feelings by causing an accident (to himself rather than to others); it could signify a plea for help, an angry reproach, a self-punishing act, a means of avoiding a stressful situation through incapacity, an acting out of self-pity.

Life events can also be a factor in accidents. Any change in life, good or bad, can put you at risk.

Life events

Some stresses are related to, or follow on, a specific identifiable event in the person's life. Attempts have been made to list life events in order of severity of their stressful impact. Death of one's spouse is usually ranked first, followed by divorce and marital separation, imprisonment, death of a close relative (especially a parent or child). Personal injury and illness, loss of employment or retirement, acute sex difficulties, and change in health of a family member come next. Even happy events such as marriage, going on holiday, a wanted pregnancy or birth of a child are regarded as having a stressful impact.

Life events which are less important in terms of stress include change in financial state, death of a close friend, taking out a mortgage, change of job or of responsibilities, and in-law troubles. Other life events related to stress are one's spouse stopping or starting work and minor offences such as traffic violations.

Some life events are unpredictable, and the person has no control at all, such as death of a spouse or personal injury; some events are brought on by the individual himself, such as taking out a loan to buy a new car.

The trouble starts when several life events hit you all at once. People are more vulnerable to stress during periods of major change. There is a finite number of changes that any individual can handle at any one time and usually the straw which breaks the camel's back is unpredictable. Therefore, where there is a predictable life event looming, you should try not to make things worse by introducing (unnecessary) other changes in your life – such as changing jobs and getting married at the same time.

The classification of diseases that doctors, particularly GPs, can use in recording their patients' diseases and problems has recently been expanded to give greater precision to diagnoses and to enable life events to be recorded; it is increasingly being recognised that illness can follow such events.

death of a close relative

Family and friends of a very ill person are under stress, too, particularly as they cannot offload their worries on to the sick person. They may have to cope with feelings of anger, guilt, sadness, helplessness (which they should not try to abate by undue fussing).

A dying person should not be allowed to be lonely but that does not mean that the living should spend weeks or months wearing themselves out in constant vigil so that they would have no strength left to cope when necessary. They should try to stay physically and emotionally as fit as possible and ready to offer comfort (if needed). The more attuned they can be to the emotional needs of the person who is facing death, the easier for all concerned. This is not the moment to try to make up for a life-time of discord.

bereavement and grief

The reaction of people to the loss of husband or wife or other close companion varies according to the circumstances and the personalities concerned. Where death has been long foreseen, perhaps after a long or difficult illness, the reaction may be accompanied by relief. This is quite normal. Where the loss is sudden and unexpected, the survivor is overwhelmed, stunned and helpless. The ability to withstand this stressful situation depends in large measure on the support given by others, and the degree to which grief and anguish can be freely expressed during the early stages.

Grief is prolonged if attempts are made to suppress its expression, particularly at the beginning, by self-imposed strictures not to give way. The bereaved person has to come to terms with, and accept the reality of, the death.

There are distinct stages in the normal reaction to grief. The first is numbness and disbelief, with the person's behaviour automatic and dreamlike. This stage is usually brief and may last only a day or so but in some rare cases will extend indefinitely. Then follows a period of prolonged depression, with painful longing for the person who has died and a desire to search for him or her, sometimes accompanied by the feeling that he is alive and near. Other people may think this is the beginning of madness; usually these feelings become less intense after a week or two. This is often followed by a time in which the past relationship is reviewed, blame apportioned for the death and perhaps responsibility laid on doctor, nurses or God. Or the survivor sinks into a state of self-reproach, often about trivial matters. This stage can go on for up to a year, but with diminishing intensity. There is then gradual recovery, shown by improvement in sleep and appetite and a willingness to start new relationships. Grief is probably never completely extinguished but is no longer a constant preoccupation.

It is important that the bereaved person should express his or her grief freely in the early stages, and should realise that any mourning process includes feelings of anger as well as sadness. A doctor's help might be sought: sleeping pills or tranquillisers prescribed by the doctor for a short time only can play a part in helping the bereaved and in minimising the immediate stress, especially after a sudden or particularly tragic bereavement.

The help of friends, relatives, neighbours with practical matters (funeral arrangements, financial support, care of children, notifications, clearing up) is also of paramount importance.

◖ **Cruse, National Organisation for the Widowed and their Children**, 126 Sheen Road, Richmond, Surrey TW9 1UR (telephone 01-940 4818) has branches throughout the country providing a service of counselling to widows and widowers, practical advice and opportunities for social contact. Where there is no local branch, there is the option of national membership with contact by letter, phone, literature, meetings in London.

◖ **The Compassionate Friends,** national secretary Mrs. Gill Hodder, 5 Lower Clifton Hill, Clifton, Bristol BS8 1BT (telephone 0272-292778) is an organisation of bereaved parents who seek to help other bereaved parents by giving them the opportunity to talk freely to an understanding and compassionate friend. The organisation has local branches.

◑ **National Association of Widows,** Stafford District Voluntary Service Centre, Chell Road, Stafford ST16 2QA (telephone 0785-45465) has branches scattered throughout the country and aims to provide help, comfort, advice and social activities for widows.

Bereavement counselling is available in some parts of the country, usually provided by voluntary associations that work alongside the local authority services. People are visited in their own home, usually once a week, for a month or two, or longer if necessary. Referrals are made by the doctor, health visitor, social service worker; people can also get in touch with the service direct. A notice about the service may be displayed in local libraries, surgeries and citizens' advice bureaux.

About 20 Widows Advisory Centres attached to and manned by volunteers from branches of the National Association of Widows offer advice on all practical and emotional problems faced by widows. Regular training seminars are held for volunteers.

illness

Illness is a major source of stress, and so is worrying about illness. This is hardly surprising in view of the major consequences of many illnesses and the fatal nature of some. However, many people have exaggerated fears about their illnesses because they do not know much about medical matters and are reluctant to question their doctors, or when they do ask are given an inadequate explanation or one they do not understand. You may have to persist in questioning. If you do not understand the answers, ask again, perhaps later, particularly if your mind refuses to take in what is being said.

Potentially fatal illnesses are particularly stressful not only because of the prospect of pain or of failing bodily functions, but because of fear of the unknown, the unspeakable. Medical or nursing treatment in which pain is not alleviated adds to the stress. When there is less anxiety about the pain itself, the severity of the pain tends to diminish.

Most people are more stressed when in pain; terminal patients who are given adequate pain killing drugs are less anxious and distressed. So neither doctor nor patient should underestimate the help that pain killing drugs can give.

The realisation of one's own approaching death is inevitably stressful, and so is the fact of dying. There may be other emotions to come to terms with: fear, sadness, guilt, anger, regret, disappointment. It can be better to express rather than to deny these feelings and to ask for help in coping with them. At this stage, the best confidant may or may not be a person who is close; possibly a more detached, friendly outsider is more able to accept the validity of what you are saying and feeling, and will not simply set out to cheer you up.

handicapping illnesses

After the acute phase of a heart attack or stroke, the person is generally left with some disabilities, both physical and psychological. The attack is usually sudden, so there is no chance to get gradually acclimatised to the idea of impaired health. Instead, a hitherto healthy person finds his life at some risk and is reminded that he, too, is mortal. Some people who find it difficult to come to terms with this realisation develop a cardiac neurosis believing that any exertion will harm them, and so become invalids unnecessarily.

Some conditions lead to permanent handicap such as blindness, deafness, being crippled. If the condition is slowly progressive, the person can adapt to some extent, so that it may not be as stressful as the sudden onset of a handicap. A chronic illness or the residual problems following an acute illness, may lead to major financial, social and personal consequences: inability to work can transform a family's circumstances for the worse. Severe stresses can be placed on a marriage, especially when the handicap is disabling. A balance has to be found between over-protecting the invalid who may find dependence on others an added stress (or become over-demanding), and risking extra dangers. Simple things, such as inability to take a holiday, may assume major stressful proportions. Sex may be difficult and a couple should not be too inhibited to seek advice over this.

Mental illness produces stresses not only on the patient but also on his relatives. For example, coping with a chronically depressed man, with some risk of suicide, may tax the resources of the most patient of wives. Living with a schizophrenic person is notoriously stressful because of his or her bizarre behaviour and unpredictability. A housebound phobic housewife may put great stress on her husband who has to do all the shopping and take time off work to stay with her if her panics become extreme. If the person who is suffering from psychiatric illness gets medical help, the benefit should extend to the patient's partner.

◑ **MIND (National Association for Mental Health),** 22 Harley Street, London W1N 2ED (telephone 01-637 0741) has local affiliated associations in London and in different parts of the country, some of which can offer group therapy and relaxation classes. Head office can give information, literature and referral to a local association.

The body's response

In the animal world, the response to acute stress or alarm (such as is produced by the appearance of a predator) is to fight or flee, or, more rarely, to sit paralysed by fear. Human reactions are not very different. All involve very rapid, almost instant changes in the muscles and organs of the body; in the fight or flight response, this may be designed to prepare the body for intense activity.

The sense organs, most frequently those of sight or hearing, receive the signal of alarm and pass it on to the brain where its significance is recognised and from which messages are sent along the nerves to the muscles and to other organs. The muscles contract, often very abruptly as in the startle response. If the state of alertness or arousal continues, muscle activity and tension remain high and render the person more capable of reacting quickly to any further stimuli.

Heart rate tends to change and increase. Everyone has felt their heart beating faster after a shock. And under certain circumstances, such as anticipation of something unpleasant, the heart may slow down and beat very forcibly. Blood pressure rises, often to very high levels, and may remain high for some time.

Blood vessels throughout the body are affected: those in the muscle open up so that more blood can course through them; those in the abdomen and in the skin contract, so that less blood goes through them. Thus, the output of the heart is diverted from skin and gut to the muscle of the trunk and limbs in preparation for greater muscular effort.

Sweating increases in fairly specific areas such as the skin around the mouth and nose, the temples, the arm-pits, between the legs and especially the palms of the hands and the soles of the feet.

The saliva dries up. Secretion of gastric acid increases, the gastro-intestinal tract is markedly affected although movements of the stomach may diminish. Sometimes the stomach becomes flabby—literally, a 'sinking stomach'. The intestines are more active and may churn and gurgle. There may be an urge to open one's bowels and, in a severe fright, loss of control may occur. The bladder is similarly affected:

there is an urge to pass water as the bladder muscle increases in its activity.

The sensory organs alter. For example, the pupil of the eye dilates, so letting in more light and functioning in a more sensitive manner.

Hormonal changes are less immediate because their speed is determined by the rate of the blood's circulation round the body. Hormones are chemical substances which are secreted into the blood stream by glands in various places throughout the body and travel in the blood stream to their particular sites of action.

Many hormones are implicated in stress responses, the most important ones are adrenaline and noradrenaline (known collectively as the adrenomedullary hormones) and cortisol or hydrocortisone (an adrenocortical hormone). Different species of animals secrete adrenaline and noradrenaline in different proportions; in man, it is mainly adrenaline.

Adrenaline and noradrenaline which are secreted into the bloodstream act on many organs, in general reinforcing the effects. Thus, heart rate increases, blood pressure rises, the pupils dilate, blood flow in the muscle increases, blood flow to skin and gut diminishes and the breathing tubes (bronchi) expand, allowing more air to be drawn into the lungs. In addition, adrenaline affects the metabolic balance of the body. It mobilises energy reserves in the liver and in the muscles themselves, making glucose available for immediate energy demands.

These changes are accompanied by changes in posture which indicate increased alertness. The person's body is in a state of readiness to respond to any further stimuli.

Each person has individual patterns of physiological and psychological response to stimuli and the pattern of responses will tend to be repeated if a stimulus is repeated. Thus, in one person the pulse rate may markedly increase each time, but there is little sweating; another person may show the reverse pattern with marked sweat-gland responses. One person's response is raised blood pressure, another's is increased secretion of gastric acid, a third shows much muscle tension, and so on.

If stimuli are repeated, the responses fall off to some extent because there is adaptation or habituation. This is a very basic form of learning – learning not to respond to stimuli which after some repetition are consciously or unconsciously perceived as irrelevant. The fall-off in response tends to be rapid at first, then tails off. It is thanks to this habituation that, for instance, after a time, traffic noises become unobtrusive to most people. However, people vary greatly in the rate at which they adapt to repeated stimuli. Some do so rapidly, ceasing to respond after a short time; others very slowly or not at all. Some unfortunates actually become increasingly susceptible: each exposure to the stimulus increases their response. Through failure to adapt, readiness and arousal are kept at a quite unnecessarily high level. It has been suggested that failure to adapt can turn into stresses many stimuli which are in themselves fairly innocuous.

When a stimulus becomes invested with a special significance, this can reverse the process of adaptation. For example, someone living near an airport may have learned not to be troubled by the noise of aircraft flying overhead. Then he reads of near-collision in the air, and becomes sensitized to the aircraft. Thereafter, he fails to adapt to the aircraft noise which then constitutes a stress for him.

Adaptation is a complex matter and its mechanism in warding off the effects of stress is not fully known. Thus, when a repeated stress no longer induces a bodily response, nor produces an emotional reaction, by definition, it is no longer a stress. Nevertheless, it is possible that the stressful circumstances are still registered by the person, even if not responded to, and this may eventually produce changes in the body. These changes are complex nervous system changes, for instance changes in sensitivity of hormonal control mechanisms.

Some bodily reactions to stress

The pattern of bodily response produced by a stress is likely to be affected by the personality of the individual: a hostile individual will produce one pattern, an anxious one another, an obsessional one yet another. Moreover, ability to express the emotion, as against keeping it all bottled up, to give vent to hostility or to seek reassurance, or to express anxiety, affects bodily changes.

Sometimes stressful circumstances can give rise to symptoms of physical distress, pain or malfunctioning.

palpitations and chest discomfort

The word palpitations means no more than that one is aware of the beating (normal or abnormal) of one's heart. This is quite usual, for instance, during and immediately after exercise. The 'resting' heart rate averages between 60 and 80 beats per minute, but the rate can rise to as high as 200 beats per minute during extreme exercise or under stress.

Palpitations can be caused by ectopic beats. These are additional contractions of the heart which make the individual feel as if his 'heart has turned over'. The majority of people who experience this quite common condition have a healthy heart; in some, anxiety or stress seems to set them off – but excessive coffee or tea drinking or alcohol and other causes may do so more often.

Chest discomfort and pain are common complaints in stressful situations and anxious people. The pain is more an ache than the constricting sensation of angina or a heart attack, or it may be a stabbing pain felt over the heart. Although these pains may be provoked by exertion, they tend to last longer than angina after exertion has ceased, but a doctor's expertise may be needed to make the distinction between these harmless symptoms of stress and those of true coronary heart disease. So, if you have any chest pains, go and see your doctor.

The combination of these harmless stress pains and such stress symptoms as tiredness, weakness, sweating, trembling and breathlessness (especially breathlessness at rest) has been given various names such as effort syndrome, disordered action of the heart, cardiac neurosis. It responds to relief of the pain, plus reassurance from a qualified person that there is no heart disease, as well as treatment directed to the source of the stress.

fainting

Some people under acute emotional stress faint: they feel light-headed and then pass out – that is, become unconscious. This is due to a change in the nervous control of the blood vessels, some of which widen, and of the heart which beats less frequently and less vigorously. As a result, the blood pressure falls and the circulation through the brain becomes insufficient. If the sufferer is laid horizontal or, while still conscious, puts his head down between his knees, he will recover in a few minutes. He should not be put into an upright sitting or standing position.

choking

Under stress, some people may suffer from a sensation of choking. Because the mouth is dry from lack of saliva and the muscles of the throat are taut, they feel that the tongue is blocking the air passage. Actually it never does, although speech may be thick and difficult. The symptom usually subsides quickly when the acute stress is relieved.

breathlessness

It is normal to feel breathless following exercise, but anxiety and stress can produce a kind of breathlessness while the body is at rest. It is a feeling of suffocation, as though not being able to get a deep enough breath into the lungs. This is often accompanied by a habit of sighing. In fact, the sufferer has usually taken in a deep breath, is afraid to let it out, and breathes shallowly and rather rapidly. He should be reassured that he will not choke and should let his breath right out and then breathe in and out more deeply, but not fast. He can then also train himself not to indulge in the tragic-sounding sighs.

overbreathing

In conditions of stress, breathing may become deeper (perhaps as more oxygen is needed by the body in its state of vigilant preparation). In some people, particularly someone who tends towards overbreathing anyway, this response can become exaggerated at times of stress. Paradoxically, they feel that they cannot draw sufficient air into their lungs, feel stifled and may flee into the open air.

The overbreathing blows off carbon dioxide from the lungs and the body, and this in turn alters the metabolic balance of the body. The nerves become over-excitable, giving rise to symptoms such as pins and needles and tingling of the hands and feet. The person becomes more anxious, overbreathes more and a vicious circle is set up. The usual emergency treatment is for the sufferer to breathe into a paper or plastic bag so that he will re-inhale the carbon dioxide that he has just breathed out: the metabolic imbalance is thus corrected. (The plastic bag must never be placed over the sufferer's head, of course.) After that, what has caused the stress response should be sought and dealt with, even though it may be trivial. This re-inhalation treatment is usually undertaken by doctors in hospitals, but a patient's relatives can be instructed to do it.

In addition to (or better, instead of) the paper bag routine, the person should be taught relaxed breathing by a chest physician or physiotherapist. People who overbreathe can be cured by learning a better habit of breathing.

good breathing

Most systems of relaxation include controlled breathing, generally deep breathing. While overbreathing under conditions of stress usually consists of breathing fast or in pants and gasps, controlled deep breathing should be slow and steady.

You should aim to fill the lower half of the lungs first, using the muscles of the rib cage and the diaphragm. Start by resting your hands against the bottom of the rib cage with the fingers lightly touching: if you breathe in correctly, you will find that your fingers will draw apart.

Hold the breath for a short while, then let the muscles relax as you breathe out. Breathing should be rhythmical and there should be a constant ratio between the time spent breathing in and the time spent breathing out.

A good position for deep breathing is to lie on one's back, with the knees half bent and the hands over the lower chest with the fingers lightly meeting. As you breathe in, check that you are opening up and filling the lower part of the lungs (by observing how your fingers are drawn apart). As you breathe out, the fingers come together again.

Another way of checking that you are breathing correctly is to put one hand on the upper part of your chest and the other on your abdomen. You can do this sitting on a chair. When you breathe in, your abdomen should expand at the start of the breath and your upper chest should not move much. Repeat this exercise several times, aiming to get your abdomen moving (as evidenced by your lower hand).

What you should concentrate on is breathing out, fully and correctly (that is, slowly and evenly); then breathe in by simply allowing the air to come in naturally, with no exaggeration or conscious effort. It is the breathing out that is associated with relaxation of muscles and can be used to assist general relaxation.

Calm controlled breathing can be used to counteract some of the stress in difficult situations, such as before an interview, an exam or a performance – or after a stressful row or a shock.

vomiting and indigestion

Some people suffer vague abdominal pains under stress. These pains are fairly diffuse, unlike an ulcer pain, and are not relieved by indigestion remedies. Make a note of when the pain comes on – it may reveal a pattern that will help to identify the source of the stress.

diarrhoea and frequency of urination

Under acute stress, such as is experienced by soldiers going into battle, overactivity of the gut can result in diarrhoea. Responding to stress with diarrhoea may happen in isolation, or it may alternate with constipation. However, these symptoms may be signs of some serious condition, and should not necessarily be attributed to stress only. If they persist, the doctor should be consulted. The bladder is another organ which increases in tension in response to stress. This results in the person having to pass urine more frequently than usual. The urge to pass urine may be very sudden and sometimes minor incontinence may occur. But incontinence may also be caused by a serious underlying illness, so if it persists you should consult your doctor.

tremor and twitching

The muscular system of the body is under very finely tuned controls. Under stress, the control mechanisms become inefficient owing to interference by impulses coming from the complex centres of the brain which govern the emotions. In addition, adrenaline can induce such changes. The result is trembling, mainly of the hands, but it can affect any part of the body. Some people who suffer from tremor at the best of times are made worse by stress and anxiety.

The trembling can be marked and disabling. Tremor of the voice muscles is shown as shakiness of the voice, or whispering. Stammering, which is a complex malfunctioning of the control and the monitoring of speech production, is made worse by stress (the details of the mechanisms involved are not known).

Twitching, another muscular stress response, may affect a tiny muscle such as one at the corner of the mouth or eye. This twitch may be so highly related to stress or anger as to be an external indicator of the sufferer's state of mind.

tension headaches and muscle aches

Muscles can go into sustained contraction during stress; amongst the most vulnerable being the muscles of the scalp, neck and face.

The basis of tension headaches is sustained contraction of the muscles of the forehead and neck. The headache is generally insidious in onset, and gets worse during the day and may even become worse after the source of stress has lessened or been dealt with. It may be throbbing in character or, more likely, feel like a tight band round the head or a skull cap pulled down hard over the temples. Taking analgesics (painkillers) usually helps, as does relaxation or massage.

Muscle tension in other parts of the body can produce a variety of aches and pains, sometimes labelled 'fibrositis' which is a vague, convenient term for ill-defined pain in and around muscles. Low back pain ('lumbago') often becomes more insistent and unbearable when the person becomes stressed. Muscle tension can usually be clearly related to stressful circumstances, and can leave the person feeling physically exhausted at the end of the day.

massage

Massage is useful in helping muscles to relax. It stimulates the flow of blood, assists in clearing away waste products from muscle cells and reduces muscular tension and associated pain.

Massage can also be valuable on the emotional plane. It is a form of physical contact between two people and can be very comforting; it reduces emotional tension and anxiety, and replaces them with a feeling of calm and trust. It can symbolise being cared for, friendship, affection and even tenderness. The person giving the massage also benefits, from the sense of touch and the satisfaction of helping someone in a direct personal way. Both parties should end up feeling relaxed and at peace.

Muscles cannot relax when cold, so it is better if the person who is being massaged is warm (and the room, too). The person who is giving the massage should not have cold hands.

Before beginning the massage, place the hands on the partner and hold them still for a few seconds, so as to transmit a feeling of calm. When the massage begins, it should not be tentative, but firm and deliberate. Do not remove both hands from the body at once, so as not to lose continuity.

As you near the end of the massage, indicate by a slight change of tempo and pressure that the massage is complete. Leave your hands lying still on your partner for a little while, so that he can come to gradually in his own time.

You can, of course, massage any part of the body, but for stress the most effective parts are neck, shoulders and forehead. You should stand behind the person and lean forward a little, while he sits on a chair with his back to you and head supported by resting against you. (Shoulder massage can be done very effectively if the recipient is lying face down.)

To massage someone whose neck and shoulders are tense and painful, or who has a tension headache, you need a combination of kneading and stroking. The stroking takes two forms: deep stroking, with pressure to counteract and ease muscle tension, and light surface stroking, which can be very soothing.

When massaging someone's forehead, both hands are placed on the forehead with fingertips lightly touching. The fingers are then moved gently towards the temples several times. After this, each hand is moved in turn straight up towards the hair-line.

self-massage

If you are on your own, you can massage your forehead by smoothing the muscles outwards towards the temples. For neck massage, it is the muscles at the back of the neck that need loosening – do one side at a time, keeping the rest of your body as relaxed as possible. It is also possible, in a similar way, to self-massage the shoulder muscles that lie over the shoulder blades.

tiredness

Prolonged stress and prolonged emotion, even when enjoyable, usually lead to a feeling of tiredness, which people may describe as feeling drained. There is considerable constitutional variation between people in the speed with which this happens. This tiredness has probably more to do with mental tension than with fatigue of the muscles or other parts of the body, although the sufferer often feels worn out physically as well as mentally. A good long night's sleep or two may be all that is needed. But if the tiredness is more severe, a period of prolonged mental rest, relaxation and diversion into other interests may be required.

insomnia

Sleep problems take various forms: difficulty in getting to sleep, waking in the night, waking early, unsatisfactory sleep.

Difficulty in getting to sleep is characteristically related to anxiety, not being able to switch off problems when going to bed; the person tosses and turns and finds it increasingly difficult to fall asleep. When sleep does come, it is unsatisfying in nature and punctuated with vivid, anxiety-provoking dreams, or disrupted by nightmares. Often the dreamer is in a frightening situation, running away and trying to escape, and he wakes bathed in sweat.

Fitful and disturbed sleep, waking frequently in the night, is typically related to depression. Waking early to the accompaniment of gloomy thoughts is also typically a sign of depression.

Insomnia due to anxiety or depression, or to stress, is unlikely to be relieved until these states have been dealt with. But inadequate sleep can be a contributing factor in stress, so it would be wise to try and tackle the insomnia directly, too.

Try to discover what lies behind your sleeping problem – and whether it really is a problem at all: laboratory tests have shown that people who believe they have chronic insomnia may be getting only about forty minutes less sleep than 'normal' people. Or you could explore your sleep problem with a relative or friend, or with your GP if he can spare the time.

In some cases, sleeping pills could be useful in seeing someone through a bad period of stress on a short-term basis. But the fact remains that sleeping pills do not do anything to deal with the cause of insomnia. For instance, some physical illnesses make sleep difficult, mostly because of pain, and it would be better to get treatment for relief of the pain; sleep should improve after treatment.

how to sleep better

Some simple measures are worth trying. Sometimes sleep is made more difficult by the environment – noise, someone else in the room, light, heat or cold. If you cannot stop the noise, try earplugs for a short time or even installing double glazing; if light comes from the street, use thick lined curtains or blinds; get the temperature right by opening windows or switching on a heater.

The body clock works to a 24-hour cycle, so it is wise to go to bed at about the same time every night and to avoid constantly changing sleep times (it may mean giving up shift-work, or frequent travel, or hectic socialising).

It can be helpful to follow a night-time routine – such as taking yourself or the dog for a walk (particularly if you have been sitting down most of the day); listening to the radio or reading (but it is better to avoid highly emotional topics, or undertaking stimulating intellectual tasks right up to bed-time); making a warm drink (but not a stimulant such as coffee or tea); locking up the house, having a bath, making sure you go to bed with an empty bladder.

There are some relaxation techniques which work by distracting you from whatever may be worrying you so that once you are in bed, your body can relax and your mind drift off. Some methods occupy the mind – for example, making up stories, word games or simple adding or multiplication games, reciting poetry. Others involve clogging the brain with boring repetition such as counting sheep. Physical relaxation exercises, such as tensing and then relaxing different groups of muscles around the body and deep breathing can help towards better sleep. Sex, too, can help sleep.

normal and abnormal anxiety and depression

An individual's personality affects his perception of external stresses and can even be a source of stress in its own right. It will also influence his way of coping with stress.

Personality is a complex aspect of a person's functioning. It is possible to highlight the predominant features of some personality traits, such as anxious, aggressive, inadequate, obsessional, and so on. However this is inevitably an over-simplification, because most people have a mixture of personality characteristics.

The two emotional responses of anxiety and depression are closely related, and are linked to stress, but not necessarily as cause and effect. As a general rule, anxiety tends to be a reaction to stressful threats, and depression a reaction to stressful losses, but many people experience a mixture of the two.

Of all the personality traits pertinent to stress, the anxious personality is probably the most important. The anxiety is never far below the surface and affects most aspects of the person's existence with a fear, often irrational, of the unknown, and anticipation of imminent catastrophe. Because the person's anxiety threshold is low, quite trivial events may be perceived as stressful. Thus, the breakdown of a domestic appliance may be magnified by an anxious housewife into a major crisis. Or an anxious man may worry over possible redundancy when he reads that the company he works for is cutting its dividend.

People vary in their predisposition towards anxiety. Most manage fairly well and do not experience undue anxiety unless the stresses in their life become too great. Many anxieties are normal in the sense that almost everyone experiences them – for example, going to the dentist, taking an important examination or being interviewed. Sometimes the worries are reactions to real enough stresses and threats: money difficulties, family problems or looming unemployment.

It is only when the anxiety is so severe, pervasive and persistent that it colours the person's every thought and feeling that it is no longer normal but becomes a nervous illness, or when worries about stupid little things become exaggerated out of proportion that the anxiety is abnormal.

abnormal anxiety states

Eventually, as the person becomes more anxious, stresses become more intense until the unfortunate individual is in danger of reacting to almost everything in his life with foreboding, tension and sometimes, in severe instances, with sheer terror.

Anxiety can become a total, overwhelming sense of foreboding, of something terrible about to happen. The worries are ever-present; the sufferer wakes up to what he feels will be a day of problems, and goes to bed with them still unresolved and preying on his mind. Tension can be felt all over the body.

The heavy sense of dread is more intolerable because of its vagueness. The anxiety is so upsetting that the sufferer becomes irritable and snappy. Anxiety interferes with attention and concentration; work, especially intricate tasks, becomes difficult. The person may feel peculiarly detached from reality as if he were looking down on himself: trying to become detached from stressful reality is a protective mechanism.

Anxiety states also produce bodily symptoms similar to physical stress responses. Palpitations, a feeling that the heart is about to stop, giddiness, faintness and unsteadiness may occur, so may chest pain, difficulty in swallowing and a feeling of a lump in the throat. Other complaints include inability to breathe, nausea, vomiting, some loss of appetite, belching, urgent calls to pass urine or stools, diarrhoea, trembling, tension headache and various aches and pains.

phobias

Some people are made greatly anxious in certain situations or when confronted by certain objects. By definition, phobia is an irrational fear that is out of proportion to the particular situation.

A common form of this is agoraphobia, in which the sufferer is unable to leave the house on his or more commonly her own, cannot travel on public transport, or go into crowded shops without becoming panicky.

Fear of objects can include dogs, birds and snakes. A person afraid of spiders may not only refuse to live in the country but to live in a ground-floor flat in town. Or a person with a fear of lifts would rather walk up endless flights of stairs.

These situations become extremely stressful to the sufferer, even when he fully realises that his fears are irrational. The person should seek medical and psychological help if the phobia is getting steadily worse or is interfering with daily activities. A short course of treatment aimed specifically at helping with the phobia can be very effective. The first step is to see the general practitioner.

◗ **The Open Door Association** c/o 447 Pensby Road, Heswall, Wirral, Merseyside L61 9PQ is a self-help organisation offering an information service. Members receive a counselling newsletter, which is a vehicle for the exchange of members' experiences and contacts.

◗ **Be Not Anxious,** 33 Broadview Avenue, Rainham, Kent (telephone 0634-34262) offers a counselling service by telephone or letter.

abnormal depressive states

The feeling of depression is a sustained mood of sadness and pessimism, despair and despondency. Sadness from time to time is normal and is understandable if things are going wrong and life just seems too much to cope with. But in some people, the feelings of depression become much deeper and more upsetting, and out of proportion to the problems in their life.

Some depressive states are obvious reactions to stress, to adverse life events, especially of loss. For example, bereavement or loss of a job can lead to depressive reactions. In other instances, the depression seems to be an over-reaction and is a type of illness, stemming largely from the person's personality. In some instances, people suffer a depression which is completely unexplained, coming 'out of the blue'.

The course of a depressive illness can vary greatly from person to person. In some people who develop depressive reactions to stressful events, the depression persists and deepens until it is unrelated to what set it off.

The prime psychological symptom of depression is a lowering of mood with a persistent and prevailing sadness. There is a lack of enjoyment of life, interests are neglected, hobbies not pursued. The person despairs of ever finding happiness and becomes downcast and lugubrious. People let themselves go, personal hygiene is neglected, clothes become slovenly. The person feels his life is worthless and unfulfilled. Minor sins are magnified into major transgressions, he feels inferior, undeserving of help or gratitude and often blames himself for his predicament. Attention cannot be sustained, concentration is poor and memory unreliable. He may become irritable and explosive and anger is only just below the surface; he may drown his sorrows in alcohol.

Bodily pain may accompany the psychological 'pain'. Headache, backache and shooting pains in the face and neck are common. People who had pains before they had any depressive episodes, find that the pains become worse. A person may become increasingly aware of his bodily functions and start to worry about constipation or breathlessness or to fear that he has contracted VD or is dying of cancer.

Bodily changes are widespread, particularly in the out-of-the-blue type of depression. Bodily function is slowed, speech becomes monotonous and unmodulated. Sleep is disturbed, with difficulty in falling asleep or fitful sleep and early wakening. Or some depressed people, usually younger ones, tend to oversleep rather than suffer from insomnia. Appetite is poor and there can be quite dramatic weight loss, with clothes hanging loosely on the scarecrow-like figure. Sexual feelings are lost and sexual performance impaired in both men and women.

◑ **Depressives Anonymous,** 36 Chestnut Avenue, Beverley, North Humberside HU17 9QU is a national organisation which brings depressives together for support and encouragement, whilst accepting conventional help.

◑ **Depressives Associated,** National organiser Mrs. Janet Stevenson, 19 Merley Ways, Wimborne Minster, Dorset BH21 1QN is a self-help service for depressives, run by ex-sufferers who have a direct understanding of the problems of depression. There are local groups which arrange meetings and activities. Where people are isolated, they are encouraged to keep in touch with others by phone or letter.

People who are depressed often experience suicidal feelings. Usually, unless very socially isolated, they communicate their intentions – however obliquely – to others. Warnings of this sort must be taken seriously. It is quite erroneous to suppose that those who talk about suicide, never attempt it.

suicide

People who attempt suicide have often experienced a major increase in stress, or a breakdown in relationships in the previous month, or other recent significant life events. In the elderly, physical factors such as pain and cancer are important precursors to suicide.

A person who feels suicidal should try to get skilled medical advice and ask to be referred to a psychiatrist. At the very least, he or she should confide in a friend, or phone the Samaritans. Talking about suicide to a sympathetic person, makes it less likely.

If you are the friend who is being confided in, take it seriously: people who threaten to kill themselves are quite likely to try to carry out their threat. Try to persuade the person to see his or her general practitioner. As a last resort, do so yourself or communicate your concern about the potential suicide to close relatives of that person.

A related but separate problem is deliberate self-harm, attempted suicide, commonly by poisoning. In young people who try self-poisoning, the act may be a protest at the treatment by someone close (such as an unfaithful spouse) or an attempt to draw attention to their own situation and distress.

Wrist-slashing is a form of self-destructive behaviour precipitated by stress. It is often carried out by disturbed adolescent girls or young women. The attempts at self-harm are usually half-hearted, leading to severe scarring rather than death, but the person should be persuaded to see the doctor and seek specialist help from a psychiatrist or a clinical psychologist.

◑ the Samaritans

The Samaritans offer a befriending service for the despairing and suicidal. It is primarily a telephone service, in some places available for 24 hours a day but this varies from branch to branch. People needing help can also call in person at one of the branches, and telephone callers who seem likely to benefit by meeting a Samaritan face to face are invited to call in. Samaritans may arrange to meet clients away from the centre during the hours when the centre is not open for face-to-face befriending. The Samaritans have around 180 centres, manned by volunteers.

The overriding aim is to reduce the number of suicides. The Samaritans are anxious to induce young people to get in touch with them instead of making an attempt at suicide or self-injury; they are also trying to find ways of making it more likely that people who have been admitted to hospital after attempting suicide will, on discharge, turn to them for help; they are also concerned that the elderly, who are a high-risk age group, should be aware of their services and avail themselves of them.

If a caller is concerned about another person, the Samaritans try to support him in his anxiety and to suggest ways of obtaining help for his friend. The Samaritans do not intrude upon people who have not sought their help directly, unless an identified responsible person informs them of the need of someone who is too young or old or ill to ask in person, in which case they may make a tentative offer of help.

Branches advertise an easily remembered local phone number and their address; they can also be found in the phone book.

The warning signs of stress

There are many signs that a person is under stress; each person tends to have his own idiosyncratic pattern of stress response so that warning signs of stress vary from person to person.

One of the most obvious and early signs of stress in another person is an intensification of personality traits. The suspicious person becomes paranoid, the inadequate falls to pieces altogether. The careful become over meticulous, the pessimistic lugubrious, the anxious panic-stricken. The irritable become explosive, the extrovert become slapdash and the introspective lose contact with everyday reality.

Some people know their own pattern of stress response, and can gauge the depth of problems by the nature and severity of their own symptoms or changes in behaviour. Stress responses involve many bodily symptoms, emotional reactions and behavioural changes and yet many people drift into situations in which the level of stress rises insidiously, and do not seem to realise what is happening.

increase in smoking and drinking

Under stress, many smokers find the number of cigarettes they buy going up rapidly; it may double over the course of a few weeks. The smoker takes great care to make sure that his supply of cigarettes does not run out; the need for a cigarette is never far from his mind. But often, cigarettes are lit and smoked avidly for a few puffs and then stubbed out in an impatient, abrupt way.

Some smokers find their habit so sensitive to stress that they can gauge the stressfulness of a situation by their cigarette consumption.

Drinking more can also be a sign of increased stress. Someone who normally takes alcohol only in the evening may start drinking at lunch time (perhaps to excess and to the detriment of the afternoon's work) to alleviate stress responses. Then he starts drinking whenever a potentially stressful situation looms, so that a bottle is kept at work and is resorted to increasingly frequently. On return home, the stressed person immediately reaches for a drink and is irritable and uncommunicative until the effects of this drink begin to dissolve the day's stresses.

appetite

Some people lose their appetite when they become stressed, anxious and depressed; others eat more when stressed, perhaps to comfort themselves. For some people, losing or gaining weight can be a barometer of their level of stress. Loss and gain of weight may, however, be caused by something more than the decrease or increase of appetite, and should not be ignored.

loss of sleep, and tension

Insomnia is a common sign of stress. Few individuals are capable of switching their problems off when they go to bed. It becomes increasingly difficult to fall asleep, and sleep is unsatisfying and disturbed, with vivid, bad dreams.

General tension and tiredness may be the cardinal signs of stress in some people. They find themselves increasingly unable to relax, being on tenterhooks all the time and unable to shut problems out of their minds. The general tension may become so great that the person feels permanently tired. There is loss of interest, loss of concentration and loss of memory, making the person seem absentminded and inefficient. Interest in sex diminishes.

inability to cope

Increasing stress may show itself as inability to cope at work. The person's performance suffers and he may flit from one task to another unable to concentrate sufficiently on any one. Increasing stress may produce a rise in general activity which may become uncoordinated or arbitrary, with much energy expended in unproductive tasks; this in turn increases the stress. The person becomes irritable and impulsive and may do unexpected and ill-considered things.

recognising the signs

A person may recognise only some of the signs of being under stress without being aware of the other ways in which stress is affecting him. He may find that he is sleeping poorly, but overlook the fact that he is smoking or drinking more; he may not appreciate that some other symptoms are also part of his stress response.

Stress can produce a tremendous variety of physical symptoms and any part of the body can be upset. Chest discomfort or pain, diarrhoea, palpitations, headaches, muscle twitches may all be signs of an increase in stress. Chronic pains become worse and more unbearable. The stressed person complains more of his symptoms and may become querulous or importune his doctor for reassurance and remedies. Multiple complaints in a hitherto stoic person may be the first sign of increasing stress.

If the stress response is not recognised for what it is and is regarded as a possible sign of physical illness, this can cause a great deal of needless worry.

your general practitioner

Seeing the doctor has become a standard way of dealing with stress problems. The doctor has to deal with all aspects of human living which vaguely impinge on health problems. The general practitioner is often the first resort of the distressed (rather than the last, as some doctors think they should be). Doctors vary widely in their attitude to their patients' stress responses and minor mental illness, from the sympathetic listener and provider of aid, to the 'pull-yourself-together' brigade.

Often a tranquilliser will be prescribed as a routine, and sometimes an antidepressant drug. This can be helpful if the anxiety response is severe or if the depression is well-established. But minor stress responses usually resolve without drugs, and tranquillisers do little to speed up that process. In most such mild cases, it is doubtful whether tranquillisers bring any benefit.

Some doctors prefer to deal with stress responses not by prescribing drugs but by counselling the patient. Findings from some studies suggest that there is much less need for prescribing tranquillisers if the doctor believes in talking to his patients, or refers them to someone skilled in counselling.

The doctor taking a proper history of the symptoms can, in itself, be reassuring and can help to put both the symptoms and the stress which produces them into perspective.

If any special tests are needed, for example to make sure there is no heart trouble, the doctor or hospital will carry them out. Reassurance that there is nothing physically wrong is powerful in reducing the additional stress which worrying about the symptoms can produce. However, many doctors prefer not to over-investigate complaints in a person who seems to be going through a period of stress. This does not mean that the doctor suspects the patient of fabricating his symptoms: he can see that it is the functioning of the organ underlying the symptom which is impaired, not the structure and substance of the organ itself.

An organ may fail to function properly without there being anything organically wrong with it and without its being damaged. This is known as functional disease, to distinguish it from organic illness in which the organ is damaged. For instance, the heart beat may be irregular without the heart being diseased. A similar kind of thing can happen with a car: the sparking plugs may fail to work not because they are faulty but because they are covered with oil (and when the oil has been cleaned off, they function normally again).

Basically, functional illness can be more easily put right. This should be particularly reassuring because it means that the stress has not done any irreparable harm. However, if in conditions such as high blood pressure or rheumatoid arthritis, stress has resulted in longer-term changes, treatment rather than just reassurance will be needed to try to remedy the structural changes that have taken place.

Some illnesses are believed to be related, at least in part, or in some individuals, to stress. In some, stress seems to be the most important factor. In others, stress is not the major factor but can make the condition worse or make bouts of illness more likely.

allergy

An allergy is an abnormally sensitive reaction to a substance which in itself is normally not harmful, called an allergen. This can be almost anything, but the most common are pollens from flowers and trees, household pets and certain foodstuffs such as shellfish and strawberries. The reaction includes hay fever, itching and a rash, nasal streaming, joint pains, wheezing. Many of the symptoms of allergy are due to the release of histamine into the blood stream.

Once something has triggered off an allergy, the person is likely to go on being sensitive to whatever substance has caused it. Treatment is generally by antihistamine drugs.

Some, but not all, sufferers find that their attacks are more frequent or more severe under conditions of stress; in some cases, emotion may be the principal factor.

angina pectoris and heart attacks

The blood which supplies oxygen and nutrients to the heart so that it can work is carried through the coronary arteries which encircle the heart. If these arteries become narrowed (by the deposition in the wall of the blood vessel of fatty substances called atheroma), the blood supply is impeded and may become insufficient. If the blood supply through the coronary arteries is inadequate when an extra load is put on it, for instance during exercise, in cold weather, or following a large meal, the sufferer may experience an anginal attack: gripping pain across the chest and sometimes into the neck and jaw or down one or both arms. When there is no longer an extra demand, such as on stopping exercise, the pain goes away after a few minutes.

Anxiety, fear and stress may bring on anginal attacks. In an emotional crisis, there is an increased release of adrenaline and noradrenaline into the blood stream, which increases the work of the heart as it beats more rapidly. The pain of the angina can then constitute a stress in its own right; the person becomes afraid of having anginal attacks. This heightened anxiety makes attacks more likely.

Drugs can be taken to dilate the arteries when an attack occurs. The drug usually used is glyceryl trinitrate (trinitrin) which is dissolved in the mouth at the onset of an attack, or the doctor may prescribe a beta-blocking drug.

When the blood supply to the heart muscle is abruptly stopped, this causes a heart attack. It is generally due to clotting in a coronary blood vessel (coronary thrombosis). Stress can contribute to this. Clotting of the blood takes place by a complex mechanism. Whatever the details, stress factors increase the stickiness of blood making it more likely to clot.

A stressful existence leads to the sustained production of the hormones adrenaline and noradrenaline. Among their actions, they mobilize fatty acids, which are a source of energy. But in the absence of exercise to burn up these fatty acids, it is thought that they accumulate and interact with other fatty substances to form an atheromatous substance which is deposited in plaques in the wall of blood vessels. (This is particularly critical in blood vessels close to the heart and in the brain and kidneys.)

the likelihood

Because heart attacks are dramatic events and doctors can monitor the changes in the electrical activity of the heart, many studies have been carried out. The results link heart attacks to a variety of psychological, physical and other factors. Diet is important, and cigarette smoking predisposes the individual to heart attacks (about doubling the risk). Gross degrees of overweight are associated with an increased incidence of heart attack. Lack of exercise is another factor, and so is too much drastic exercise. Probably it is the interaction of factors – heredity, diet, high blood pressure, smoking and stress – which is important.

Attempts have been made to relate the likelihood of a heart attack to personality types. Two american researchers, Friedman and Rosenman, divided their male subjects into two groups: type A people with a chronic sense of time-urgency, are aggressive, ambitious, driving themselves on to meet (often self-imposed) deadlines. They are self-demanding, often doing two or three things at once, impatient and always in a hurry. They are likely to react with hostility to anything that seems to get in their way and are temperamentally incapable of letting up. They are also likely to think they are indispensable. All this adds up to a state of constant stress.

Type B men exhibit opposite characteristics, being less competitive, less preoccupied with achievement, less rushed and generally more easygoing, not allowing their life to be governed by a series of deadlines. They are also better at separating work from play and know how to relax. They are less prone to anger, and do not feel constantly impatient, rushed and under pressure.

The incidence of heart attacks was much higher in type A than in type B individuals. A and B are not strict prototypes but indicate patterns of behaviour shown by certain people in our society. Most people are not straight As or Bs but a mixture, with type A or B predominating.

asthma

In an attack of asthma, the tubes through which air is carried in and out of the lungs become narrowed by contraction of the muscles in the wall of the tube and also by the secretion of a sticky mucus in the tubes themselves. It therefore becomes more and more difficult to get air into and out of the lungs. The symptoms are shortness of breath, wheezing and cough. The worse the breathlessness, the greater is the feeling of anxiety, which in turn may worsen or prolong the attack.

Although the cause of the disease is not fully known, something is understood about what triggers individual attacks of asthma. Attacks can be precipitated by allergies, chest infections, irritant gases, and psychological factors. The balance between these is not clear cut and varies from person to person and from time to time. Stress does not 'cause' asthma, but in some people it is the initiating factor; in others, stress is the factor which prolongs the attack. Often it is a combination of factors that produces an attack.

Possibly, stress brings about a change in the bronchial mucosa and in the pattern of breathing; genetic factors may contribute to maintaining a disturbed pattern of breathing behaviour.

If stress can cause, or contribute to, attacks of asthma, reducing stress should be of benefit.

There is evidence that training in relaxation, not repressing anger and not panicking when minor changes in breathing occur, reduces an asthma sufferer's attacks.

The old belief that over-anxious mothers contribute to their children's asthma has not been scientifically substantiated. But where psychological factors such as the parent's over-protectiveness or the child's using attacks to get attention seem relevant in a child's asthma, family counselling may help to lessen the degree of stress.

◑ **Asthma Society and Friends of the Asthma Research Council,** St Thomas's Hospital, Lambeth Palace Road, London SE1 7EH (telephone 01-261 0110) has local branches which hold meetings and offer help and information to individual sufferers and their families.

baldness

Alopecia is acute baldness in which hair falls out in handfuls. Not only can the scalp hair fall out, but eyebrows and bodily hair as well. The alopecia may be localised, so that the person develops bald patches. The cause of alopecia is uncertain. Some sufferers can relate it to episodes of stress, especially in initial attacks, but in other people the connection is less clear. The hair may suddenly grow again.

cancer

In spite of a great deal of research, much remains to be discovered about the cause of cancer. It is probable that, like heart trouble, cancer has no single cause and that there are a number of risk factors. The more of these factors apply to a person, the greater the likelihood of cancer. A theory which is being followed up by researchers is that emotional factors, such as stress, could be a contributing factor in some cancers. So, cancer is beginning to be seen as one of the diseases in which the functioning of the body may become affected by physical changes associated with disturbed mental and emotional processes. (It could be that people who are prone to depression are more susceptible, particularly people who repress their emotions. Breast cancer, in particular, has been linked to life-long repression of anger and hostile feelings.)

If emotional factors do, indeed, contribute to the development or course of some kinds of cancer, such an effect must be brought about by biological mechanisms. It has been suggested that the body's immune responses, which defend it against cancer cells, may be impaired by stress. Stress induces secretion of adrenaline and noradrenaline and it is possible that these hormones, in turn, tend to suppress or reduce certain immune responses. However, it is highly likely that many complex mechanisms are involved; the biological pathways linking emotional factors with cancer remain to be discovered.

The possibility that stress and personality characteristics play a contributory role (albeit a small one) in certain cancers raises the question of whether psychological methods of treatment can help to improve the outcome. Various techniques have been tried including biofeedback, hypnosis, psychotherapy and so-called visualisation in which patients learn to imagine their white blood cells attacking and destroying cancer cells. Doctors who recommend these techniques do not intend that they should take the place of conventional treatment, but that they should be used in a complementary role. Claims for the efficacy of psychological treatments should not be accepted uncritically.

diabetes mellitus

It seems doubtful whether diabetes can actually be caused by physical or emotional stress. However, acute symptoms may occur for the first time following physical illness or injury or an emotional upset. So, it may be that a stress can bring into the open diabetes that was hitherto hidden, rather than provoking diabetes in a previously normal individual.

In people already under treatment for diabetes, both physical and emotional stress can cause a worsening, but individuals vary greatly in their susceptibility. Physical stresses (infections, heart attacks, accidents) can provoke the symptoms of untreated diabetes, in particular thirst and excessive urine flow. Less is known about the effects of emotional stress. Where it is followed by worsening, this may be due as much to the person's reduced attention to the details of the treatment regime as to a direct effect on the body metabolism.

Diabetic adolescents, in particular, may react against the restrictions of the treatment regime or may, consciously or unconsciously, use their diabetes as a weapon in their relationships with other family members or with people outside the family.

Like any chronic disorder, diabetes can give rise to emotional stresses, usually when the diagnosis is first made.

◗ **British Diabetic Association,** 10 Queen Anne Street, London W1M 0BD (telephone 01-323 1531) has 300 local branches and groups of friends which hold meetings, arrange educational holidays for young diabetics and visits for the elderly.

◗ **National Diabetes Foundation,** 177a Tennison Road, London SE25 5NF (telephone 01-656 5467) has local branches and a 24-hour answering service, particularly useful for the newly-diagnosed and parents of diabetic children; it does not give medical advice. Can help with stressful family situations, pregnancy, diet, etc; runs holidays for diabetic children and welfare services for the elderly.

high blood pressure (hypertension)

There is evidence that periods of stress are associated in some people with a rise in blood pressure. In most cases, if the stress is removed the blood pressure will revert to normal. However, if the blood pressure rise has been severe and prolonged, changes can take place in the arteries of the body which result in raised blood pressure being maintained even after the stress has been reduced or removed.

High blood pressure is associated with many other effects. When the pressure is high, the heart has to pump harder, putting it under strain. Oxygen supply to the heart muscle may become insufficient, resulting in anginal attacks. Hardening and narrowing of the arteries is more likely, and this in turn can produce heart attacks and strokes: the high pressure can burst blood vessels, resulting in brain haemorrhage. The kidneys may become affected by the high blood pressure to the point of failure. Thus, raised blood pressure is a major health risk, cutting down life expectancy quite appreciably.

Blood pressure may rise and become abnormal without any symptoms being noticed. But if you suffer from headaches, or unexplained fatigue and dizziness or palpitations, it is worth consulting your doctor.

Raised blood pressure is by no means necessarily due to stress. But a person suffering from high blood pressure should examine his life style and attempt to change it if it is stressful. This will help the person even if the blood pressure does not respond.

irritable bowel syndrome

This condition, also called spastic colon or irritable colon syndrome is very common but has only recently been widely recognised. The symptoms are colicky pain, usually in the lower abdomen, variable bowel habit with periods of diarrhoea, constipation or both; distension of the abdomen, and occasionally belching or heartburn. Symptoms can come and go over long periods of time, and are often made worse by stress.

One theory is that irritable bowel syndrome may be caused primarily by a lack of residue in the diet. By the time the remnants of food, after absorption of nutrients, enter the colon (large bowel) they have insufficient bulk to be propelled easily downwards to the back passage. Instead of the small contractions required to squeeze a large bulk down the bowel, the colon has to squeeze very tightly to propel a small bulk. This may lead to spasm of the colon, which causes the pain; the lack of bulk produces either diarrhoea or small hard pellety stools. Stress can make the colon go into spasm, particularly if it contains insufficient bulk and this exacerbates irritable bowel syndrome.

Drugs that relieve colonic spasm are sometimes prescribed at first but generally irritable bowel syndrome is treated by trying to deal with sources of stress, and by increasing the fibre content of the diet. This is best achieved by eating plenty of green vegetables and wholemeal bread, and by taking bran either as a bran-enriched breakfast cereal or as raw unprocessed bran. Raw bran is dry and tasteless but is palatable if mixed with any food – three tablespoonfuls daily is sufficient.

In two less common diseases, ulcerative colitis and Crohn's disease, the bowel becomes ulcerated. The symptoms are attacks of diarrhoea containing mucus and blood; both diseases usually continue for years with attacks often precipitated and exacerbated by stress. Treatment, usually under hospital supervision, involves the use of steroids and some other anti-inflammatory drugs. Obviating stress can help a great deal in avoiding frequent attacks.

migraine headaches

Although the term is sometimes used indiscriminately to refer to any severe, prostrating headache, migraine is a specific type of headache due to spasms and relaxations of blood vessels in the coverings of the brain.

The attack usually starts with visual phenomena (called an aura) which can take the form of flares around objects, or flashes of zig-zag patterns. The headache is severe, usually accompanied by nausea and vomiting, and great sensitivity to light. The pain usually affects one side of the head only.

The mechanism of the attack is believed to be a constriction of the blood vessels supplying the brain followed by a dilatation. The first is supposed to produce the aura, the second the headache.

Some sufferers recognise that their attacks are closely related to episodes of stress and tension in their lives. Relaxation techniques may help these sufferers and so may non-prescription analgesics. Otherwise, treatment is mainly by drugs containing ergotamine which constricts the dilated blood vessels. It is helpful if the sufferer can sit or lie down in a quiet, dark room and, if possible, sleep.

◖ **The Migraine Trust,** 45 Great Ormond Street, London WC1N 3HD (telephone 01-278 2676) encourages and assists research into migraine. It publishes a booklet on migraine and a news sheet and can also give advice over the telephone.

Sufferers from migraine can attend the Princess Margaret Migraine Clinic, Charing Cross Hospital, Fulham Palace Road, London W6 8RF (telephone 01-741 7833). They should first obtain a letter of referral from their doctor and then telephone or write for an appointment. Anyone who has a severe attack while in the vicinity of the clinic can at any time receive emergency treatment. They should ask for the casualty department and will be directed to a room where they will be seen by a doctor especially interested in migraine and where they can rest quietly.

A similar service is offered by the City of London Migraine Clinic, 22 Charterhouse Square, London EC1 (telephone 01-251 3322).

In the provinces, a number of hospitals have an interest in migraine. Sufferers could ask their doctor to refer them to the department of neurology. The Migraine Trust is able to advise as to which hospitals have this particular interest.

◖ **British Migraine Association,** 178a High Road, Byfleet, Weybridge, Surrey KT14 7ED (telephone Byfleet 52468) is a voluntary organisation aiming to further research into migraine and its treatment, and to keep its members informed of new advances. It offers a postal and telephone information service.

pain

Pain is a subjective sensation, which can be affected by previous experience of pain, and can become genuinely much worse when a person has other causes for anxiety, such as worry about illness or physical disorder. An upset in personal relationships, job worries, a bereavement, or being under financial pressure can affect the symptoms. For instance, backache can become worse as a result of psychological stress, such as anxiety, and other social and emotional pressures.

Tooth clenching and grinding are stress-related habits; prolonged contraction of the muscles involved can cause headache and facial pain that seems like toothache. (Opening your mouth by about half an inch and pressing down the jaw against the pressure of a hand held under the chin, and then letting it drop normally, can help to counteract the tension of various facial muscles. Try doing this for a few minutes each day, preferably in the evening before going to bed – but if the pain persists, go and see your dentist.)

Prolonged persistent pain can itself be a profoundly disturbing experience and very stressful. If it goes on long enough, it may disturb the normal pattern of behaviour.

Some people can tolerate a lot of pain and others only a little. Under stress, some of us may become anxious, hypochondriacal or depressed. Minor physical complaints may be magnified in the person's mind, consciously or unconsciously, until they produce a quite disproportionate disability.

peptic ulcer

A peptic ulcer is a breach or defect in the lining of the upper part of the gut. Peptic ulcers are most common in the duodenum (the first part of the small intestine), but can also occur in the stomach (gastric ulcer) and the gullet (oesophageal ulcer). The commonest symptom of a peptic ulcer is pain.

Many people with a gastric ulcer find that food makes their pain worse; those with a duodenal ulcer often find that their pain is brought on by hunger and relieved by eating. Pain from any type of ulcer is nearly always helped by milk or an antacid.

A person may have typical symptoms and yet have no ulcer. The diagnosis can be confirmed in an outpatient clinic by an X-ray examination after drinking a 'barium meal' or by fibre-optic endoscopy in which the doctor examines the inside of the stomach through a flexible telescope.

The causes of peptic ulcer are different for each type of ulcer. Acid appears to play a leading role. The stomach usually produces a strong acid but protects itself from being digested by this acid by secreting a coating of mucus. Stress increases the secretion of acid and decreases the secretion of mucus.

Food neutralises gastric acid and it is during long periods of stressful work on an empty stomach, that the acid begins to damage the lining of the stomach, and an ulcer starts. Alcohol, particularly spirits taken on an empty stomach, further damages the mucosa. Smoking probably increases secretion of gastric acid and may interfere with secretion of mucus; it therefore contributes to the formation of ulcers and slows their healing.

Some drugs (most of which are available only on prescription) can cause a peptic ulcer. Aspirin and anti-inflammatory drugs used in the treatment of arthritis are the worst offenders. Aspirin can be bought over the counter, on its own or contained in one of a large number of patent medicines – some for the relief of dyspepsia. Anyone suffering from dyspepsia should read carefully what is contained in a medicine, to make sure that the list of ingredients does not include aspirin. Be warned by 'salicyl . . .' in the name; for instance, sodium salicylate, salicylic acid, acetylsalicylic acid.

An antacid, in liquid or tablet form, relieves pain by neutralising gastric acid. Taken regularly in sufficient quantities for long enough an antacid can heal an ulcer. It is, however, surer and more convenient to be prescribed an ulcer-healing drug, of which there are a number. The doctor's choice depends on factors such as the site of the ulcer. A full course of such treatment lasts four to six weeks and almost always heals an ulcer.

Ulcers often return unless the conditions that encouraged the ulcer in the first place are changed. It is therefore important for the person to consider the sources of stress in his life and whether they can be removed or at least alleviated. Often a change of attitude is called for, or a change in life-style. Stopping smoking, regular meals (frequent and small rather than few and big) and the avoidance of spirits are important; these habits are usually easier to change when stress has been reduced, as the two are often linked. The details of a diet are probably less important than is popularly thought, but it seems sensible to avoid fried, fatty or highly spiced food, and anything which seems to cause pain.

premenstrual tension

Disorders of menstruation such as premenstrual tension can both cause, and be influenced by, stress. During the few days before the onset of menstruation, the woman feels physically and mentally fragile, anxious and irritable, and stressful circumstances are coped with less well.

rheumatoid arthritis

A feature of this disease is a proliferation of inflammatory tissue in the membrane which lines some of the joints of the body, especially the hands and feet, wrists, elbows and ankles. It produces swelling, pain and stiffness of joints and can become disabling.

The specific cause of the inflammatory reaction is not fully clear. It seems likely that the body's immune mechanisms which normally play an important part in the defence of the body against disease are disturbed so that they are activated by some of the body's own protein, producing destruction and inflammation. Research is going on as to whether, how and why the body's immune mechanisms react in this destructive way in rheumatoid arthritis.

It is possible that stress is one factor involved in altering the normal immune mechanisms. Animal experiments have demonstrated how stress can affect immune response.

There may be a link between stress and the onset or worsening of rheumatoid arthritis, but this is difficult to prove. In a recent study it was found that in the three months before onset of rheumatoid arthritis, the women affected underwent significantly more stressful life events than a control group of women.

skin diseases

Skin diseases which, although not primarily of emotional origin may to a greater or lesser extent be aggravated or perpetuated by stress, include urticaria (nettle rash or hives); itching without obvious skin disease, often in the anogenital region; acne, especially the particular form in which picking and squeezing at the lesions perpetuates them and produces the typical excoriated appearance.

Atopic eczema is a disorder with an inherited tendency towards itchy dry skin, areas of redness and tiny blisters which break to produce crusts. The condition may be associated with asthma or hay fever. Scratching leads to scabs and to thickening of the skin, which in turn leads to further itching. Atopic eczema commonly gets worse at times of emotional stress, for example, exams, entry to a new school, the birth of a sibling.

Psoriasis is also an inherited disease. The visible signs may come and go spontaneously; they are red, scaly patches, usually affecting the outer surfaces of elbows and knees, the scalp and back, sometimes affecting the nails to produce gross thickening. Various factors may provoke psoriasis, including, in some people, stress. The emotional stress caused by psoriasis is often one of the worst features of the disease.

Emotional factors and stress are important in the development, aggravation and perpetuation of many skin diseases, and the stress and misery caused by the skin disease may lead to a vicious circle. An awareness by friends, relatives and the general public that skin disease is seldom contagious, that it is not dirty, that it is not the sufferers' fault and that it causes them great embarrassment, would help to reduce the stress caused by skin disease and make the treatment of it easier.

◑ **National Eczema Society,** Tavistock House North, Tavistock Square, London WC1H 9SR (telephone 01-388 4097) aims to encourage research into eczema and to spread information about it and its management;

there are nationwide groups which meet for talks and discussions and exchange of information.

◖ **The Psoriasis Association,** 7 Milton Street, Northampton, NN2 7JG (telephone 0604-711129) is a self-help association which aims to encourage research into psoriasis and to spread information about it; there are local groups providing social contact and mutual aid and support.

tricks of the mind

There are some involuntary mental mechanisms for warding off stress which are not consciously recognised by the person.

Adaptation is learning not to respond to repeated or continuing stresses and stimuli when the response has become futile or even damaging. It is a major defence against stress.

Other ways of dealing with stress, which are less satisfactory and permanent than adaptation, derive from the inability to face unpleasant reality and may contain a degree of denying or distorting reality. These mechanisms are similar to some everyday mental processes, in an extreme form; the difference is one of degree rather than of kind.

Denial means quite simply persuading oneself that something is not so, in the hope that it will not be so. If we tell ourselves that problems do not exist, perhaps they will go away. If we shut our eyes so that we cannot see something, perhaps it is not there.

To deny that anything is amiss or needs facing up to is one way of trying to deal with stress. The person denies the existence of problems and difficulties whenever they are raised by others, and most of all he denies them to himself, in an attempt to safeguard his emotional security or self-esteem. He may succeed in dodging the stress for the time being. But relationships with others are likely to suffer and may be irretrievably damaged through the person's persistent refusal to acknowledge that problems exist. Friends, relatives, colleagues and anyone else involved with the person are often left feeling frustrated or angry. However, they can help by making it as easy as possible for the denier to change his stance without losing face – not saying 'at last you are seeing sense, you fool' but 'I think you may have a point there' as a starting point for tackling the hitherto-denied problem.

Rationalisation is a means of self-deception by which a person finds satisfactory and socially acceptable reasons for conduct. Rationalisation comes into play in a 'sour grapes' situation when someone who fails in his objective then claims that the prize was not worth having. A man who fails to gain promotion may minimise stress by asserting that the promotion would have had so many disadvantages that he is better off as he is. Sometimes the spouse will collude with this rationalisation, in which case harmony is maintained. If the spouse refuses to enter into the deception, this may create another source of stress.

Projection is the attribution of personal shortcomings and failures to the environment and other people, as exemplified by the bad workman blaming his tools (and the incompetent executive blaming everyone but himself for his failures). In a more extreme form, projection can become paranoia, the person becoming deluded in his blame of others.

Displacement is the diverting of emotional emphasis from one object or person to another. Displacement activities include the enthusiastic espousal of a hobby when promotion is blocked at work or when there is marital friction.

Displacement activity can take the form of biologically inappropriate activity when an appropriate one is blocked, such as banging one's fist on the table instead of into the rival's face, kicking the cat instead of one's spouse.

Withdrawal is more passive – the stressed person throws in the sponge and attempts to retire emotionally from the situation by daydreaming and becoming apathetic. The stress no longer elicits any response, but nor does anything else.

Partial withdrawal is seen in nostalgia, where the stressed person reverts to the past, usually forgetting the unpleasant things and dwelling on his past successes. Many old people succumb to this, as their way of coping with the stress of having no future.

Regression is a more complete reversion, not just to the past but to an earlier childhood state. Under stress, even robust personalities may yearn to return to a state of dependency in which they were protected and decisions made for them. Sometimes this regressive tendency is actively encouraged. Hospitals are notorious for this, nursing and medical staff conniving with relatives in rendering the patient passive and dependent. Most patients quickly acquiesce, only a few refusing to surrender their adulthood: they are then labelled 'difficult'.

In some cases, the stressed person becomes very hostile and aggressive. This is also a way of trying to deal with stress but it results in much wear and tear on the stressed person and on those around him.

aggression and hostility

People under stress become short-tempered and irritable, resenting questions and snapping back. Hostility is sometimes not shown towards the person at the root of the problem but as displaced aggression towards someone else, who becomes the scapegoat. This is likely to happen if the source of stress is a person in a position of power or superiority, such as one's parents or boss.

Aggression can take a physical form. Wife-battering is a form of assault resulting from aggressive impulses. It has a long history and is still regarded by some men as acceptable behaviour and by some women as a fact of life. Sometimes, the aggression is a form of sexual release or precedes sexual intercourse. In other cases, the aggression stems from stress or provocation. The frustrations of unemployment, straitened circumstances, unwanted children lead to venting of aggression on the woman. (Occasionally, the roles are reversed.)

Baby battering is not a new phenomenon; doctors have become alerted to the fact that unusual or repeated injuries in babies and children may not be accidental. Battering parents may themselves be perpetuating a cycle of reacting to stress and problems with physical aggression.

Parents may find themselves becoming increasingly irritable and snappy because of tiredness and shortness of sleep. If they become exasperated with the baby or child they should try to take turns at minding the baby, and should try to agree between themselves on what line to take with the child so as not to add to the stress by additional discords.

The support of one's family and friends should not be underestimated. It is worth trying to keep lines of communication open with family and friends who often worry but dare not approach for fear of being rebuffed for interfering. Give them a sign; and try to make use of the informal family/friend network for sharing and unburdening problems.

People who use trusted friends and relatives with whom to talk over problems can relieve much of the stress and tension they may be feeling. Others may use the health visitor or anyone who does not seem too eager to leap in with advice, but is ready to listen.

◑ **Women's Aid Federation (England),** 52–54 Featherstone Street, London EC1Y 8RT (telephone 01-251 6429/6386), provides temporary accommodation in refuges to women and their children who are suffering physical, mental or sexual abuse. Can be contacted by phone on a 24-hour service.

For Scotland and Wales, the head offices are **Scottish Women's Aid,** 11 St. Colme Street, Edinburgh EH3 6AA (telephone 031-225 8011) and **Welsh Women's Aid,** Incentive House, Adam Street, Cardiff (telephone 0222-462291). The address for Northern Ireland is **North Irish Women's Aid,** 143a University Street, Belfast 7 (telephone 0232-249041).

◑ **Family Network** is a phone-in help service for families, organised by the National Children's Home, 85 Highbury Park, London N5 1UD, to assist with problems such as family violence, battering of wives, child abuse, drugs. It operates in many areas and the telephone numbers of regional services can be obtained by writing in or by telephoning 01-226 2033 (in office hours only).

◑ **Parents Anonymous (London),** 6 Manor Gardens, London N7 6LA (telephone 01-263 8918), has parent volunteers who provide a telephone helpline, offering a listening ear to parents in distress. They may also visit people who have asked for help and accompany them to see the doctor or when in search of professional help. Similar groups exist elsewhere sometimes under names such as **Parent lifeline,** or **Families under stress.**

◑ **Organisations for Parents under Stress,** 21 Chadfield Road, Duffield, Derby (telephone 0602-470551 ext 505) is a co-ordinating body under the umbrella name OPUS that can give parents the phone number of a group in their part of the country.

If there are organised groups in the community, take advantage of them – mother and toddler groups, young wives', church, drop-in centres, self-help groups – places where you find others with similar difficulties; it helps to know that you are not the only one.

Choosing a confidant

Talking over problems and sharing one's worries is probably among the most useful and positive therapeutic steps that anyone can take. Sometimes just putting fears or emotions into words makes them clearer and more easy to come to terms with and makes difficulties fall into their proper perspective.

Someone who would be the right confidant for one type of stress may be inappropriate or even disastrous in other circumstances. For diffi-culities at work, a spouse may be ideal to discuss things with; but a wife who has consistently undervalued her husband's abilities is not going to be much use in discussing dispassionately with him his feeling of failure at being passed over for promotion. Conversely, if she has always regarded him as unfairly held back in the promotion stakes, she may add to his sense of grievance, just or unjust, and not help an objective assessment of the present difficulty.

For marital problems, it may be better to talk to someone other than one's spouse, at least to begin with, until the nature and extent of the problem have been fully realised.

The more neutral the confidant, the more useful. There must be mutual faith and trust, and honesty rather than play-acting. In general, the role of a confidant is less that of giving advice than of letting the other person talk and offload some of the worries; solving some of the problems is only incidental. Some people have the useful knack of just allowing a stressed person to talk, hardly intervening except for an encouraging word, murmur or nod to continue.

Close friends can be useful in discussing general problems and some-times there can be a reciprocal give-and-take of help and advice. However, one must beware of the barrack-room lawyer, or the instant pundit or the self-styled expert, always ready to take over the lives of others. If specialised legal, financial or medical matters appear to be involved, a lawyer, accountant, bank manager, or doctor should be seen and their advice sought. The citizens' advice bureau is staffed by people experienced in giving practical advice and in searching out the problems in any particular case.

Some people are delegated to act as counsellors as part of their job. Personnel officers employed by large companics, although not primarily there to help people who feel stressed, can be useful confidants. They are also able to help in practical ways, especially if the stress stems from work situations. Other colleagues at work may be helpful but if the stress stems from problems at work, the situation may be delicate. Junior colleagues may be embarrassed at being regaled with a senior person's problem. Immediate superiors have the prime responsibility for the welfare of their staff, but are also liable to be a source of stress and thus inappropriate. So it is generally preferable to seek the advice of someone at the same level or more than one step above.

Traditionally, ministers of religion are delegated by society to deal with the problems of their fellow men. But fewer and fewer people profess themselves to belong to any organised religious body, so not many people avail themselves of this source of help.

The doctor may find the role of confidant thrust upon him, especially where the stressed person has developed worrying bodily symptoms for which he seeks reassurance and relief. Unfortunately, many doctors are ill-trained to act as counsellors or under too much pressure to assume what they may regard as a non-medical role. They may focus on the symptoms, play down the general stress problem and prescribe tranquillisers.

personality factors and the confidant

Different types of people tackle the talking over of stress problems in different ways. Personality traits affect people's choice of confidant, how they articulate the problem, how receptive they are to suggestions, to what extent they are able to view the problem dispassionately, and so on.

Anxious people may feel reluctant to discuss their problems and may prefer to sweat it out (often literally) on their own. Once the initial resistance is overcome and they find they have a sympathetic listener, they benefit greatly from reassurance.

Closely related to the anxious personality is the personality trait of obsessionality. The person fixes an idea into his mind and mulls over it to the exclusion of other things. Any external stress will be magnified severalfold because of the continuing ruminations. The person may be constantly checking things such as gas-taps being turned off or windows locked. In general, obsessional traits show themselves as excessive tidiness, inability to see the wood for the trees, over-attention to detail and illogical and often time-wasting strategies for doing things. In extreme cases, people may develop rituals such as washing their hands seven times before each meal; or specific fears, for instance of harming other people.

Obsessional people may chew over their problems ad nauseam and it is only a very patient listener who does not become bored with their constant preoccupations. The confidant may have to be directive and take control of the conversations, making the person keep to the point. Obsessional people are helped by being made to list their problems in order of priority because their personality makes them give every stressful circumstance equal weight.

Introspective individuals may not mull over matters in such an obsessional way, but every event is pondered, both for its implications and for its emotional and intellectual impact. Potential occurrences may be rehearsed in advance so that every activity of life becomes intellectualised and stress can become magnified by concentrating on its potential impact.

A related but different personality trait is that of the dreamy individual who elaborates events into a rich imaginary life. This can lessen stress by insulating the person from reality, which is transformed into fantasy. A more extreme version of this personality trait is the withdrawn who has opted out and avoids stress by refusing to allow it to impinge on him. He is protected by his detachment, and by his minimal involvement in life. Such withdrawal may follow a stressful experience as an attempt to cope with it.

Once introspective people feel confident in their confidant, they may talk very clearly and with insight about their problems. They tend to welcome a listener because they find that the more they agonise over a problem of their own, the more indecisive and confused they become. But the really withdrawn and dreamy individuals find talking to other people difficult. The would-be confidant may feel that it is impossible for the withdrawn person to communicate properly and may give up in exasperation. It is essential to try to focus the discussion on to points of reality.

The paranoid individual is guarded and suspicious and sees danger lurking around every corner. He may be touchy and irritable about things but the stresses are often imagined or exaggerated. Relationships with other people are strained and this is usually the main source of stress; he tries to reduce stress by blaming others.

To a paranoid person, who is prickly and hostile, any attempt to help may seem a threat, any refusal to help a rejection. Great patience and perseverance are needed by the confidant until the sufferer begins to trust someone. The art is to tread the narrow tightrope of not appearing either a persecutor or an ally. Very consistent handling is necessary because the paranoid person is very sensitive to imagined slights.

Another personality trait is that of the passive rather inadequate person. Instead of withdrawing from stressful experiences, the individual allows them to wash over him like waves on the seashore. He does not attempt to oppose stresses and allows them to encroach, and then absorbs them without apparent response.

The passive or compliant person seems easy to help because he takes advice readily, but he may be too lacking in drive to follow advice about positive action. The danger is that he becomes over-dependent on the confidant or that the confidant becomes too directive and starts to live his life for him. This temptation must be resisted.

The aggressive individual is basically truculent and hostile, with a chip on his shoulder. He is opposed for opposition's sake and not necessarily because something or someone is wrong. He has little concern for the feelings of others and tramples people underfoot. He generates his own stresses in his dealings both with things and with people. Aggressive people often respond badly to stress which tends to make them more hostile, often in an undirected way.

The aggressive person seeks advice in a positive way but usually does not act on it, unless it confirms his own ideas. Only if things go very wrong and the aggressive person becomes chastened, does he become amenable to discussion and advice.

The word neurotic as a personality trait is usually applied to people who show excessive behaviour characteristics and exaggerated or over emotional responses. Almost by definition, neurotic implies abnormally high susceptibility and reaction to stress. The person with neurotic personality traits is possibly the most difficult type of person to act as confidant to. The unpredictability of behaviour is such that it can be difficult to identify the source of stress, especially as misleading clues abound. What appears to be the source of stress may be innocuous and what appears neutral or even supportive may be stressful to the person. The confidant should be wary of getting too involved and keep his emotional distance if the problem is major or has been present a long time. But neurotic people easily become dependent on others and may not be easily rebuffed. They then become a source of stress for the poor confidant, perhaps tormenting him with the alleged ill-effects of following his advice.

no miracles

It is no good hoping for an instant identification of problems when talking them over with a confidant. The difficulties should be pondered and discussed on two or three occasions and tentative conclusions arrived at. In searching for factors which have led to stress responses, it is important not to jump to facile and hurried conclusions. Some rough record or diary can be kept to try and see whether the stress responses do follow particular identifiable circumstances. If the sufferer himself, rather than the confidant, can reach the tentative conclusions, so much the better. Just being able to talk about the problem, conclusion or none, can be a source of support.

identifying the source of stress

It is important but often difficult to recognise the true and relevant sources of stress; much effort can be needlessly expended in trying to neutralise or remove wrongly-presumed sources of stress.

Stress in one circumstance may spill over and influence another situation. For example, a man stressed at work may come home in an irritable, explosive state, so that domestic friction arises. Domestic friction may lead to preoccupations and inattention at work, and poor work performance, putting the job in jeopardy which increases the marital problem. The factors interact and stress builds up from both. Trying to tackle them means first sorting out which of them is the original cause and how they interact. Unconscious defence mechanisms of the mind, such as rationalisation or projection, may need to be brought to light first.

previous coping

The stressed person should try and work out how he dealt with similar problems in the past. If he coped in the past, he should ask himself (or his confidant) 'Why am I not coping now?' The answer may help him to identify the problem. The stress may be greater, more persistent or mean more to him. For example, threat of redundancy is much more stressful to a man when he has a family to support than when he is a footloose bachelor. The stressed person may find it more difficult to cope because of several untoward happenings in quick succession, or physical ill health, or greater age.

Previous coping may have involved behaviour which the stressed person can no longer use. For example, he may have blamed others for his deficiencies at work but finds that this excuse no longer works. Sometimes, stress has been borne with the help of a particular person, relative or friend, who is no longer available. In reality, they were doing most of the coping for him and without their support, the person cannot function.

counselling

Counselling can help people to identify their sources of stress by putting into words their fears and anxieties and then to adjust to them, or else to adjust their circumstances.

Counselling may be on an individual or a group basis. The main disadvantage of group counselling is that individual problems cannot be discussed in confidence. The advantage is that the members of the group can give each other support and advice – and it is economic of professional time.

Not many doctors carry out more than brief counselling, but every regional health authority has a psychological service. Non-medical counsellors, usually clinical psychologists or social workers and trained lay-people such as marriage guidance counsellors, are available to help people both within the NHS and privately.

The aim in counselling sessions is to give factual information to the person and to set him individual goals, allowing him to tackle his sources of stress. Factual information is down-to-earth stuff, such as whether a divorce is feasible, how much it would cost to move house, and similar things. How this information is received and used is important – to both the counsellor and the client. Counselling is best seen as reality-orientated, dealing with the here-and-now, helping with current difficulties. It may involve an hour a week for 3 or 4 weeks.

Psychotherapy tends to be more intensive and more prolonged and is intended to uncover some of the symbolic transactions which are producing neurotic responses, such as an adult reacting to another person as if he were still a four-year old reacting to his parent.

The most intensive form of psychotherapy, namely psychoanalysis, involves 4 or 5 hourly sessions a week for a year or more and is the province of highly specialised practitioners, medical and non-medical, who have undergone a prolonged training.

During psychoanalysis, the patient recalls with his therapist earlier key relationships. In this way, disordered behaviour patterns which are self-destructive or inappropriate, which generate misery, can be identified and gradually corrected as the person becomes conscious of them. A dazzling, single discovery of 'the cause of all the trouble' is very unlikely, and is not the aim even though this popular misconception is remarkably persistent.

◖ **Westminster Pastoral Foundation,** 23 Kensington Square, London W8 5HN (telephone 01-937 6956) offers a range of counselling services including individual, group, marital and family counselling. The most appropriate service for each person is assessed with them at their first session. Those who seek help are expected to contribute as their means allow but no one is denied help if they cannot pay.

There are affiliated services in other towns and in other parts of London.

◖ **The British Association for Counselling** at 37a Sheep Street, Rugby, Warwickshire CV21 3BX (telephone 0788-78328) can put people who feel in need of counselling in touch with a counselling service or with individual counsellors who are members of the association.

Helping oneself

Learning to cope with stress should be a gradual, planned process, rather than an ephemeral enthusiasm or an obsession which itself becomes a stress. No simple measure is likely to be a cure-all which will lead to a state of blissful happiness, nor, however, should any measures be thought futile without giving them a chance. Removal of even a minor problem can alleviate stress quite suddenly, leaving the person in a better position to cope with major problems.

Ways of reducing stress can include changing oneself or one's relationships, changing one's activities, and leading a healthier life. Many of these changes will interact; for instance, change of attitude is likely to change one's relationships with others.

change of attitude

As far as stress is concerned, how people see themselves is more important than the reality of their situation and is a major factor in coping or not coping. Stress responses are largely determined by, for instance, the perceived threat to emotional security or to self-esteem. Thus, changing the perception of the stress – how one views it – can mitigate the effect of the stress or neutralise it completely.

towards happiness

One activity which should be modified – although this appears at first sight to be negative advice – is that of trying actively to pursue happiness. A 20th century myth is that 'happiness' should be actively striven for. This sets up unreal expectations. Much unhappiness, discontent and sense of futility can be avoided by modifying one's attitude towards the more sensible goal of avoiding or removing known sources of unhappiness, rather than consciously trying to pursue happiness.

Another will-o'-the-wisp is the belief that 'Once such-and-such is out of the way, I shall be happy', because then another obstacle will occur to postpone this state of utopia. It is better to try and analyse the reasons for the present discontent, and then decide whether you have to make the best of a bad job or can do something to alter it.

Rather than blaming the past for our present difficulties and inadequacies, it should be examined for lessons it can give us about dealing with problems in the future. Nor should one dwell too lovingly on the past. Comparing the present with 'the good old days' is a recipe for discontent and stress, because the mind forgets the bad things and views the good through nostalgic rose-tinted spectacles.

towards aspirations and ambitions

Many people set their expectations too high so that when, inevitably, some goals are missed and there are no outstanding achievements, a sense of failure and futility sets in and ordinary problems become magnified to stresses.

People's aspirations vary enormously from the brash individual who wants to conquer the world to the diffident, self-effacing type who truly believes that the meek will inherit the earth. When ambition drives a person on, to beyond his capabilities, stress will mount as the realisation dawns that the goals are unattainable. Even worse than unattained ambition is slipping back, demotion, with loss of status and therefore loss of self-esteem. A sense of failure and worthlessness may then follow. In Japan, where 'face' was traditionally so important, suicide might have followed the disgrace of failing in one's job and ambitions.

Resetting goals realistically and re-assessing achievements as modest but worthwhile, should lessen the sense of inadequacy. A realistic view of your strengths and your own shortcomings (usually more apparent to others than to yourself) is an important step in reducing stress. It is difficult to be rational and honest about one's own shortcomings, so be prepared to listen to, and not reject without thinking, other people's assessment of your capabilities. The unattainable should be recognised for what it is, so that realistic goals can be set and pursued.

towards recognition

To many people, acclaim is more important than they would admit, and failure to achieve it may not only hurt but turn into stress.

An actor is obviously gratified by applause but, in order to carry on, he has to learn to assess the worth of his own performance and to give himself the necessary recognition, and appreciate his own achievement. When you are satisfied with your own performance, you should not need to be told by others how good you are in order to enjoy and appreciate what you have achieved. Where praise does come from outsiders, savour it, as an actor would applause.

Knowing what a pleasant thing praise is, if you, in your turn, admire something that someone else has done or achieved, say so – being told may be the one bright moment in that person's day.

towards the Joneses

'Keeping up with the Joneses' is a self-imposed scourge, and only too common; attempting to outshine them can lead to great stress. The fact that the competition is self-imposed in no way diminishes the stress.

To some extent, television encourages Jonesmanship by setting criteria for what seems like success in life and arousing unreal aspirations and encouraging goals of materialism and status-seeking.

Glossy advertising is accused of raising hopes and ambitions to stress-making levels: the accent on acquiring wordly goods reinforces the idea that you are a failure if you do not possess whatever goods are being held out as the norm for the Joneses.

towards how much it all matters

Some people only begin to cope with stress when they finally accept that much of life is full of uncertainties. If you can cultivate an ability to stand back, and view your activities in as detached a way as possible, you may be able to learn to distinguish between difficulties of your own making or capable of being lessened, and those which are immutable.

When you realise what is truly beyond your control, you can stop trying to alter it.

Activities and emotions which seem terribly important to the person involved at the time, may seem ridiculous viewed from another angle. Petty rivalries at work or bickering in the family which might build up into stressful situations can be defused by a sense of the ridiculous and the absurd: try and envisage, for instance, what a visitor from outer space would make of a domestic row.

priorities in relationships

Support from the family is a most important protection against the effects of stress. It is therefore particularly important that conflicts within the family should be resolved, if this mutual support is to be achieved.

Some people overvalue outside relationships and priorities, such as work and career ones, and undervalue the real most personal relationships: those of husband/wife, child/parent, close friends – people for whom one can do something directly and personally. You cannot change the whole world and make it a better place, but you can help to make your family and immediate circle of friends a happier one. Finding something or somebody to care about helps to give a sense of purpose. But be careful not to invest new friends, new goals and new sources of interest with a magical or overrated significance.

doing something

Through the media, we get to know about matters that are outside our control and are yet a source of concern and worry; this helplessness is a source of stress. Many people have general fears for mankind in the nuclear age. Those who actively campaign for sanity and survival and join activist groups, for instance to protect the environment, may or may not achieve the major goal, but may feel less stressed by going out and trying to do something about it (plus the solidarity of like-minded spirits) than those who just sit and worry.

Helping others is a worthwhile (and incidentally stress-reducing) activity. But even if it is done as voluntary work, it should be disciplined and done on a regular basis. Visiting an old lady or two when the whim occurs may help neither the visitor nor the visited.

Community activities and projects may be available, for example helping to clear and reclaim waste land for a children's playground. Initiating such a project, or opposing bureaucratic schemes, or agitating for a by-pass road to prevent a village being pounded by heavy lorries, enables some people to find a purpose in life. But such displacement activities should not be allowed to take over as a new source of stress.

Regular leisure activities are important in reducing stress. After all, not all one's time is spent on work and people should make time for positive leisure pursuits rather than, say, spending 2–3 hours each evening watching television. The spare-time gardener whose vegetables may not win prizes but which can be eaten, the amateur photographer whose prints may not be displayed in the local library but are admired by the family, the cyclist who does not do untold miles a day but discovers out-of-the-way villages, get much satisfaction from their activities. The satisfaction often comes from doing rather than from the results. Someone taking up painting, for example, should not be discouraged if a still-life turns out looking like an abstract. The interest should be in the activity.

Group activities are usually more stress-reducing than solitary ones, because the social aspect of meeting new people can be stimulating. Groups of enthusiasts usually welcome someone new who wishes to take up 'their' hobby and may offer the use of equipment so that the newcomer can make sure he really has an interest before laying out money on it.

Adult education institutes run day and evening classes and the list of subjects available in the larger centres is often staggering in its length and variety. Local hobby groups often display advertisements in the local library, civic centre or the local newspaper.

Increasing social contacts can lessen stress by widening one's interests. Even throwing a party puts stress into a different context. Getting out of social isolation may need effort and one must be prepared to give more than one receives – which is not always easy when going through a rough patch oneself, but worth the trying.

religious activities

To some people, the most supportive of group activities is active participation in religious practices, ranging from occasional acts of worship and prayer to complex codes of conduct governing relationships between man and man, man and his environment, and man and his creator. The common theme is of a system of beliefs, beyond formal proof, held by a group of people.

The support given by a religion is compounded of the existence of a corpus of shared beliefs which transcends rationality and can lend meaning to life, plus the feeling of belonging to a group of like-minded people.

Pressures to conform may, however, be extreme in some of the more highly organised religious denominations and sects; if the person conflicts with the group beliefs, or challenges the authority of the established religious figures, he may be excluded from the group. This loss of support and alienation can be very stressful. But, in general, if the spirit of the religious beliefs is adhered to, stress can be markedly alleviated.

As well as spiritual support, many religious organisations provide practical help, and many charities are linked to religious bodies. Some churches organise relief for the needy of the locality and are open much of the day on an emergency basis.

Many people, who are otherwise irregular in their observance, turn to religion at times of bereavement and personal crisis. The ritualisation of the burial ceremony can help people to come to terms with loss. Many ministers of religion, even if unworldly and unable to help with many practical matters, are experienced in counselling the stressed and will not refuse help if it can reasonably be given.

keeping a pet

Judging by the number of dogs depositing ordure on our pavements, cats howling at night and the astonishing variety of other animals in our homes, keeping a pet is one of our national pastimes.

Many people remark how relaxing a pet can be. Certainly, a disdainful cat who refuses to be hustled into doing anything against its wishes and the unquestioning loyalty and affection of a dog can each illustrate some fundamental values in life.

Because the relationship with a pet is relatively stable and uncomplicated, keeping a pet has been advocated as helpful for mentally distressed people when convalescing after an acute breakdown.

A dog has the added advantage of needing to be taken for walks, played with, and taken care of to a greater extent than that independent creature, the cat. But even a cat curling up on your lap asking to be stroked, or sitting by the fireside and making the room feel lived-in, can help people to relax during periods of stress.

But do not expect too much from your pet or treat it as if it were a child. And if the pet does not meet your needs, do not lose interest in it and leave it to fend for itself.

Improving your health

Improving your health in general can help lessen the effects of stress on the body. Everyone knows how minor infections multiply when you are feeling run down, and how chronic aches and pains become magnified.

Some commonsense measures to improve general health include not smoking, eating a sensible diet, getting proper sleep, taking regular exercise and cutting down on excessive alcohol. In strict moderation, alcohol probably does more good than harm in alleviating mild stress. However, moderation is the key word. Taking alcohol solely to alleviate major or prolonged stress is a way of dealing with only the symptom and not with the cause. Moreover, there is the threat of becoming dependent on alcohol if it is used as a way of tackling problems.

smoking, drinking, drugs

A person under stress may attempt to cope by using chemical means – nicotine, alcohol, drugs – to lessen the symptoms or increase his ability to withstand the pressure.

cigarettes

Youngsters begin to smoke out of curiosity, to conform to the usages of a group to which they want to belong, to appear rebellious, to appear more grown up. People continue to smoke for one or more of the following reasons:
– stimulation, for a sense of greater energy and vitality
– ritual, for the satisfaction of handling the paraphernalia of smoking
– pleasurable relaxation, as after a meal or sex
– habit, being almost unaware of taking a cigarette
– boredom, for something to do while waiting for someone or something
– reduction of stressful feelings such as tension, anxiety and anger
– dependence, having to continue so as to prevent the unpleasant craving which stopping smoking produces.

The two most important factors are the two last ones, and there is a close relationship between them.

Nicotine produces a complex series of changes in the body, including the release of adrenaline and noradrenaline, as in stress. So, smoking compounds the bodily effects of stress.

Cigarettes may help to lessen the emotional impact of stress, but at far too high a toll in medical consequences. The role of cigarette smoking in producing heart disease and lung cancer is well-known but widely ignored by smokers.

Attempting to stop smoking is a major stress, particularly when physical dependence has developed. Heavy smokers are aware of increase in anger or irritability as they try to stop (and their spouse notices the increased irritability in them for some time). Withdrawal symptoms include restlessness, anxiety, drowsiness, fatigue, insomnia, inability to attend and to concentrate, tremor, palpitations and headache. The craving may go on for weeks or months, and sometimes, though not inevitably, one cigarette can induce total relapse.

◗ **Action on Smoking and Health (ASH),** 5–11 Mortimer Street, London W1N 7RH (telephone 01-637 9843) issues free pamphlets about giving up smoking and lists of local authority smoking withdrawal clinics. Local health education officers can also guide people to clinics in their area.

◗ **National Society of Non-Smokers,** 40–48 Hanson Street, London W1P 7DE (telephone 01-636 9103) operates a walk-in information and advice centre and organises regular smoking cessation courses.

alcoholism

Alcohol is widely used for its effect on mood. It is ultimately a depressant not a stimulant; its immediate effect is to remove inhibitions and lessen anxieties and fears. A small amount facilitates social gatherings, makes the introvert person more extrovert, and makes people more assertive, self-assured and aggressive.

Whether a person will drink in a particular situation, and how much he will drink, is determined by a number of factors, including how stressed the person feels at the time. There is no such thing as a clearly-defined alcoholic personality. What leads a social drinker to lose control and become a problem drinker or an alcoholic varies from person to person. Family factors are important; occupation affects the likelihood of alcoholism – publicans, actors, seamen and doctors have a high death rate from cirrhosis of the liver.

Some people drink for enjoyment or to be sociable; others – clearly stress-related drinkers – in order to allay anxieties and depression. The alcoholic may drink as a response to stress but his state of dependence is itself a major stress, creating a vicious circle. As a person becomes psychologically and then bodily dependent on alcohol, the threat or reality of withdrawal symptoms complicates the picture: the alcoholic drinks to prevent these symptoms. Withdrawal symptoms include shakiness, sweating, anxiety and depression; the severe syndrome is delirium tremens (D.T.'s) with its terror, confusion and visual hallucinations.

◑ **Alcohol Concern,** 3 Grosvenor Crescent, London SW1X 7EE (telephone 01-235 4182) publishes a leaflet which gives places where help is available and promotes a range of services for problem drinkers and their families; it can refer people for counselling.

◑ **Alcoholics Anonymous,** P.O. Box 514, 11 Redcliffe Gardens, London SW10 9BQ (telephone 01-352 9779) is a voluntary worldwide fellowship of people whose joint aim, mutually reinforced, is to attain and maintain sobriety. There are no fees, the only requirement for membership is a desire to stop drinking. The programme is one of total abstinence, based on staying away from one drink one day at a time.

In the UK, over 1900 group meetings are held every week. AA does not provide drying out or nursing services or sanatoriums, nor can it offer domestic or vocational counselling, or welfare and social services. AA numbers are given in local telephone directories and can often be found in the 'useful numbers' section.

◐ **Al-Anon** Family Groups, 61 Great Dover Street, London SE1 4YF (telephone 01-403 0888 24-hour service), is a worldwide organisation to help relatives and friends of problem drinkers, whether or not the problem drinker seeks help or even recognises the need to do so. There are over 700 groups in the UK. Anonymity is strictly preserved. Members attend group meetings which are a form of group therapy in which they share their experience and learn the facts about alcoholism as an illness and what they can do directly to help themselves and indirectly to help the sufferer.

◐ **Alateen** is a part of Al-Anon with separate groups especially for young people, aged 12 to 20, who have an alcoholic parent, brother or sister.

◐ **Accept** (the name stands for Alcoholism Community Centres for Education, Prevention, Treatment and Research) Accept Clinic, 200 Seagrave Road, London SW6 1RQ (telephone 01-381 3155) provides team community services and treatment centres for problem and dependent drinkers and their families. Treatment is free and confidential. **National Drinkwatcher Network** groups and clubs are being established for mild problem drinkers and to educate the public in sensible drinking habits.

Contact with Accept is normally made individually or through doctors, social workers, employers or voluntary organisations.

tranquillisers

Currently, the most widely prescribed drugs in this group are the benzodiazepines such as diazepam (Valium), chlordiazepoxide (Librium) and clorazepate (Tranxene) during the day, and nitrazepam (Mogadon) at night. They calm people down and make them feel brighter and more able to cope and make their problems seem less insistent.

However, taking tranquillisers for stress reactions does not of itself deal with the stress. If a patient goes to the doctor with a stress response that is caused by a problem and is treated with tranquillisers, the problem is merely shelved, not solved. In many cases, the person will eventually have to do more than just take drugs.

Tranquillisers are not free of drawbacks. They may cause some drowsiness and can dull sensitivities and after prolonged dosage lessen intellectual capabilities. Evidence is now building up which suggests that some people become dependent on benzodiazepines in that they experience unpleasant withdrawal symptoms when they try to discontinue their drug. The price of tranquillity may therefore be a form of dependence.

However, in cases where anxiety is excessive and disabling, the risk of dependence is worth taking if the relief helps the person to resume a normal occupational, social and marital life. And if the drug is discontinued gradually and under medical supervision, the withdrawal symptoms can be much less nasty.

◖ **TRANX (National Tranquilliser Advisory Council),** 17 Peel Road, Wealdstone, Harrow, Middlesex HA3 7QX (telephone 01-427 2065) offers self-help groups for people who want to overcome their addiction to minor tranquillisers and sleeping pills; one-to-one counselling; advice and information concerning withdrawal symptoms.

◖ **Accept** (see page 103 for address) can offer free and confidential treatment to people misusing tranquillisers.

◖ **Release** (see page 106 for address) keeps a register of self-help groups and can refer people to individual groups.

drugs of dependence

The causes of dependence are complex. In some people, the relaxation and escape from stress in the drug-induced state lead them to repeat their initial drug 'highs'. Eventually, when psychological or physical dependence has become established, the habit may be maintained partly because of the wish to induce a drugged state but also, in the case of the opioids, to prevent withdrawal symptoms. When the need to procure further drug supplies dominates the addict's life, this is a further major stress.

Drug taking is often something kept secret and it may be impossible for an observer to do more than hazard a guess. In some cases there may be very little objective evidence, especially in the early stages, unless someone happens to see the person at a time when he is actually under the influence of the drug or in a disturbed condition. If a person can admit that he has a drug problem, his general practitioner can refer him to the local psychiatric clinic or, in some localities, to a specialised clinic generally called an addiction centre or drug dependence clinic or drug dependency unit. Some centres also accept self-referral, without a general practitioner's intervention.

In some cases, the person will be offered admission to hospital where the drugs will be gradually withdrawn and other drugs given to alleviate the withdrawal distress. The process takes up to a few weeks and during that time the person's general state of health, which may be poor, will also receive attention. In some centres, attempts at withdrawal on an outpatient or day-patient basis are made.

In many cases, withdrawal from the drug is only the first stage, followed by longer-term rehabilitation at a special centre, or in hospital, where some of the underlying problems that lead to drug abuse are treated.

◗ **Standing Conference on Drug Abuse,** (SCODA), 1–4 Hatton Place, Hatton Garden, London EC1N 8ND (telephone 01-430 2341) is an umbrella organisation for the different voluntary bodies concerned with drug misuse and can refer people to sources of personal advice and counselling.

◗ **Institute for the Study of Drug Dependence** at the same address, (telephone 01-430 1991), can give information on all aspects of non-medical use of drugs and on the risk of dependence attaching to drugs. It can also advise on risks and side effects of drugs and on their legal status. It cannot offer individual help or counselling.

◑ **South Wales Association for the Prevention of Addiction,** 111 Cowbridge Road East, Canton, Cardiff CF1 9AG (telephone 0222-26113) offers a nationwide 24-hour telephone counselling and advice service.

◑ **Release,** 1 Elgin Avenue, London W9 3PR, (telephone 01-289 1123 or 603-8654) can assist with information on drugs and the law relating to drugs, and with referrals for treatment. They can advise on problems with tranquillisers. Basically, the service on offer is initial counselling and referral.

◑ **Narcotics Anonymous,** PO Box 246, London SW6 (telephone 01-871 0505) is a fellowship of people recovering from addiction, following a recovery programme on the lines of Alcoholics Anonymous.

◑ **Families Anonymous,** 88 Caledonian Road, London N1 9DN (telephone 01-278 8805) is a self-help organisation for the families and friends of drug abusers (based on the principles of Alcoholics Anonymous). Arranges weekly discussion meetings.

sport and leisure

Exercise and sport are excellent ways of lessening stress and of preventing some of its damaging effects on the body. Also, sleep at night tends to be sounder following exercise during the day. Exercise can range from a long walk in the country to a brisk game of football or squash. It can be taken irregularly, perhaps when stresses begin to mount up, or, better, as a regular routine. However, sport and exercise must be relaxing if they are to serve as safety valves against stress, and should not be used as a displacement activity and invested with a special significance, lest they, in turn, become a stress.

Instead of alleviating stress, leisure activities may add to it if the person is inherently competitive. Some joggers doggedly insist on their 5 miles a day, whatever, and become stressed if they fail to attain their goal. Worries over golf handicaps or how well the team is doing can become exaggerated.

In general, leisure activities act as a safety outlet, but compulsively attending every play at the local repertory theatre, or attending bingo every tuesday night may add to rather than lessen stress.

holidays

Taking holidays is important. A holiday lends perspective to problems and they can be seen for what they are. Even if you do not go away, having a holiday at home, perhaps with day excursions, is a stress-reducing manoeuvre.

Do not be too ambitious in what you attempt on holiday so as not to turn what should be a relaxing, regenerative experience into a major expedition, that produces its own stresses. For instance, a self-catering or camping holiday may be no relaxation for the chief cook and bottle washer; nor may too much driving for the chauffeur.

In planning a holiday, it is important to identify the purpose realistically, for instance to determine whether sightseeing or sun-worship would be best, or how to combine the two. Holidays that are overly planned, or reduced to a schedule, tend to be less relaxing than unstructured spontaneous activity (or passivity).

Some people thrive on unplanned breaks, others find the impulsiveness of such holidays stressful and like to know exactly when their holiday will occur (and to look forward to it). Some lucky people have regular holidays once or even twice a year, and punctuate the rest of the time by long weekends. Some townspeople travel into the country every weekend, cycling or walking or visiting historic homes and gardens, when a longer holiday is impossible. Travel and holidays are still good bargains in terms of stress reduction.

Learning to relax

Stress-reducing procedures which can be learned include relaxation, meditation and yoga, self-hypnosis and autosuggestion, biofeedback and coping in imagination. They have many elements in common, and people vary as to which they find most helpful. If one type of approach is unsuccessful or helps only a little, another may be more acceptable and useful.

People should not feel deterred by the suggestion that they might try meditation or yoga or some other of the stress-reducing strategies that need practice: you do not need to become highly proficient in order to derive benefit. It is similar to a person setting out to learn to play the piano – even if he will not become a virtuoso, his own small achievements will give him a greater joy in music generally.

progressive relaxation

Mounting tension in our muscles is often the first sign that stress is increasing. Muscle tension and mental tension go hand in hand, the state of mind and the state of body each reinforcing the other. Learning how to relax the body can help relax the mind.

learning how to do it

The overall principle of progressive relaxation is that each of the main muscle groups in the body is tensed, held taut and then relaxed in turn, until the whole body is relaxed. The idea is that before you can relax your body, you must learn how your muscles feel when they are tight and tense. Letting go after tensing gives a physically pleasant feeling in the relaxed muscles. Developing this awareness of the difference between muscle tension and muscle relaxation is essential. It can be quickly demonstrated by clenching the hand into a fist, and holding it tight for a little while – then letting go, and appreciating the feeling of release. The same is true if you hunch up your shoulders, stay that way, and then let all the muscles go.

You should allow at least a quarter of an hour a day to practise relaxation, and try to follow the same sequence every time. It is best (at least at first) to choose a quiet dimly-lit room where you can be warm and comfortable and not subject to distractions. Relaxing surroundings are helpful but not essential. Remember that relaxation should be enjoyable, otherwise it will not work. Begin by taking off your shoes and loosening any tight clothing, especially at the neck and waist. Adopt a relaxing posture: the easiest is probably lying down, although sitting is also all right. (You can practise in an armchair – and in time you should be able to relax even in an office chair or on a bus or in the driver's seat of a parked car, or wherever you happen to be.)

Attending a class, with a live teacher, is probably the best way to learn. It is also possible to buy tapes or records giving instructions for you to follow, or you may be able to get hold of some written instructions which a friend or relative could read out to you. Alternatively, you could yourself record the instructions on to a tape and play it back when you want it.

Lie down on a carpeted floor or a bed, provided it is not too soft. All parts of your body should be supported comfortably. Lie with your arms and legs a little apart. It is better to do without a pillow, if you can.

You should tense and relax each part of your body in turn, starting either with hands and arms, then head and down through the trunk to the legs, or starting with the feet and legs and working up through the body.

If you begin with the hands and arms, you should first clench the fists, which also entails clenching the forearm muscles. Hold this for a little while, perhaps 10 seconds, and feel the tension; then let go and feel the difference – a sensation of welcome release. Then hold the hands (fists clenched) against the shoulders so as to tense the upper arms, feel the tension, and then let go.

The neck can next be held taut with the chin pressed in, then relaxed, followed by the different facial muscles – forehead (frown and relax), eyebrows (raise up then release) eyes, mouth (purse up and release) jaw (thrust forward and release), then the shoulders (hunch up then let go), stomach, buttocks, thighs, legs and feet. Each time you should consciously feel the tension before you let go.

After tensing and relaxing each muscle group in turn, you should feel relaxed all over. Instead of thinking of yourself in parts, be aware of the whole body and if you feel any remaining tension anywhere, try to release it – if necessary by first deliberately tensing the affected muscles, and then letting go.

Allow 5 to 10 minutes at the end in which to enjoy your relaxed state. You should be breathing quietly, with slow, shallow and gentle breaths. You may want to imagine a peaceful scene, for instance lying peacefully by the side of a blue lake, with green grass and trees, the song of the birds, the warmth of the sun, your body warm, heavy and relaxed. Choose your own imagined scene – whatever you like best.

When you are ready to get up, first have a good stretch, then either sit up very slowly or turn over into what is called the recovery position (turn on to your side, draw up the upper arm until it makes a right angle with the body and bend the elbow, draw up the upper leg until the thigh makes a right angle with the body and bend the knee, extend the underneath arm backwards with the hand against the buttock – all this is infinitely simpler than it sounds), then get up.

staying relaxed

Your aim should be to carry over your relaxed state into whatever activity follows your period of relaxation.

Once the technique of relaxation has been learned, it should be possible to relax without first tensing all the muscles and it should be easy to detect any areas of tenseness and quickly release the tension in these areas.

Throughout the day, get into the habit of checking whether you are tensing any muscles unnecessarily. If you are, you are not only wasting energy and effort but could well bring on headache, neckache, and backache. As muscle tension can be the cause of headaches and backaches, it follows that these can be avoided or eased through relaxation.

If your face is tensed and mouth turned downward, relax it and consciously force the corners of your lips upwards into a smile. It may be mechanical, but helps you to feel less dejected or stressed.

yoga

In this country, many people practise hatha yoga which consists of postures, movements and breathing exercises. They do this mainly because it makes them feel good, relaxed, and physically fit.

Teachers of yoga call it a way of life that people practise in order to find new avenues of spiritual development. The postures and the breathing techniques are designed to exercise the whole body systematically, and are said to improve the circulation of the blood throughout the body. The physical changes associated with all forms of yoga help to reduce stress. The aim of the discipline is that the mind, too, should become free from everyday tension.

Although yoga can be learned to some extent from books, it is better to attend a class, at least to begin with, if only to be shown the right postures – and for the encouragement of practising in the company of others.

Most local authorities offer yoga and relaxation classes as part of their adult education programme. Local newspapers and yoga and leisure-activity magazines carry details of classes, both subsidised and private.

Alexander method

Teachers of this method of posture training, which sets out to correct faulty movements and postures, start by noting and correcting the pupil's characteristic patterns of body misuse and his faulty posture habits, which are creating physical and mental tension. The pupil is taught to recognise and apply the best pattern of movement and posture for him, and is then able to practise the method as a self-help technique. Students of the method find themselves gradually adopting better physical postures and also unwinding mentally.

◑ **The Society of Teachers of the Alexander Technique,** 10 London House, 266 Fulham Road, London SW10 9EL (telephone 01-351 0828) will, on request, send a list of teachers of the technique.

meditation

Many schools of meditation have developed or been adopted in the west and some extravagant claims have been made. But simple meditation techniques have been shown to reduce stress responses in many people.

During meditation (and probably during other stress-reducing techniques) oxygen consumption and depth of breathing decrease, heart rate slows down and the brain waves assume the pattern characteristic of relaxation, while mental alertness is unimpaired. The nub of the procedure is to focus attention very narrowly, either on a specific object such as a flower, or on a special word (a 'mantra') which is repeated in imagination. The person sits quietly engaged in this simple monotonous activity. He is thus essentially doing nothing, in itself a relief from the pressure of everyday life. He must let his attention be focused without that itself becoming an active process. Meditating is attending to that focus.

When a distracting thought drifts into consciousness, the mind should be gently led back to the chosen word, sound, or visual symbol.

The environment should be relaxing – a quiet room, dimmed lights, no telephone to ring unexpectedly. The meditator sits (or lies) in a comfortable position; clothing should be comfortable and unrestricting. Meditation for about 10–15 minutes twice a day is about average. Once a person knows how to do it, even a couple of minutes' meditation at any time can help to counteract the build-up of stress.

Meditation classes are available at many adult education centres. Some experienced practitioners are happy to give private or group lessons but it is important that they do not abuse the trust of their pupils by making extravagant claims – or charging extravagant fees.

Although the technique is easy to learn, meditation may not have immediate appeal. This is because it involves doing virtually nothing and this does not come naturally to people in our culture. The whole process may at first seem too passive. It is also important for people not to attempt to assess their performance in the art of meditation as, by definition, they cannot do this and at the same time meditate.

autogenic training

In autogenic training, you lie or sit in a quite place and are taught to repeat phrases which suggest that particular parts of the body are getting heavy and warm and that the mind is at rest. This should induce deep relaxation and reduce stress and make a person respond more readily to positive autosuggestions.

Conditions which have been known to respond to autogenic training include some stress-related disorders. However, people who have suffered from heart trouble, stroke, high or low blood pressure, epilepsy, diabetes or been under psychiatric treatment, should not try the method without first consulting their doctor.

Sometimes people who are learning the method may find that when they are in a state of deep relaxation they recall distressing episodes from their past. Reliving these old traumas can be a useful experience because it allows the person to release pent-up feeling which may have been contributing to his stress. But people are strongly advised to train under the supervision of a doctor or psychotherapist (individually or in small groups), so that the recall of distressing experience can then be handled with the help of the therapist. Attempts to 'learn' autogenic training therapy from commercial tapes are likely to achieve little, or even produce worrying experiences.

hypnotherapy and self-hypnosis

In the hypnotic state, control of the mind is not given up to the hypnotist. Nor is hypnosis in any way a form of sleep: it is a waking state of altered awareness, in which the person focuses on a set of suggestions and allows himself to be receptive to them.

In the treatment of anxieties, continuous suggestions of relaxation are given by the therapist, interspersed with getting the person to imagine stress-producing situations. This shows the subject that he can remain calm and controlled while visualising various stresses. Subsequently, should any such situation arise in the course of his daily life, the person will have learned to deal with it, without stressful reactions reappearing.

In the hypnotic state, people accept suggestions that lessen their tension and anxiety and they can be instructed to get better from their illness, or gradually to improve their disturbed behaviour. Nowadays hypnotherapy is taught in some medical schools and is used by some doctors, dentists and clinical and research psychologists. There are also lay hypnotists who may be without medical knowledge. It is not excessively difficult to hypnotise someone, but only a trained person knows what to do next.

Doctors who use hypnosis teach their patients self-hypnosis so that they can at a time of stress immediately produce in themselves a relaxed and altered state, free from anxiety.

People can learn to hypnotise themselves without any outsider. But it is easier, and generally better, to start with a medical teacher.

To succeed with self-hypnosis, you need an open mind, genuine motivation, time, and a quiet place and an effective set of hypnotic suggestions. Beware of trying too hard: the aim is to feel relaxed, and receptive to suggestions from within or from without.

The most widely used method for inducing a hypnotic state is to select a stationary object (preferable one requiring the eyes to turn upwards and so inducing a certain degree of fatigue) and fix your attention on it. You should tell yourself that as you look at it, your eyelids will get heavier and heavier until they close and that at that point you have reached a state of relaxation and full awareness. Repeat this suggestion at intervals of about a minute. Concentrate on the heaviness of your eyelids until they close. Become aware of your breathing. Take a deep breath, hold it, then breathe out slowly, saying to yourself 'relax'. Let your breathing be slow and regular. Deal with any residual tension you may be feeling by saying to yourself that you will relax more deeply every time you breathe out.

The second phase is concerned with deepening the hypnotic state. This is achieved by slow, deep, breathing and the help of any visual imagery that can suggest a sense of downward or upward movement. (You can come out of even a deep hypnotic state at will with a count-down, in which you tell yourself that you will surface after counting to 5.)

You can then proceed to suggestions concerning your behaviour, thoughts and feelings, formulating resolves to change in various ways. In later sessions, you will be reiterating these as necessary, by way of reinforcement, and you may be formulating new ones. What you are doing is to foster in yourself a feeling of control over yourself and your environment.

Suggestions are more effective if they are repeated and phrased positively ('I shall . . ', rather than 'I shall not . . .', avoid also 'I'll try . . .', which suggests that you might fail). Visual fantasy images in which you picture yourself doing what you say you are going to do are often even more effective than verbal suggestions.

coping in imagination

Something that we have all done at some time, namely rehearsing how we will deal with a particular situation, can be deliberately practised as a stress-reducing manoeuvre. It involves confronting, in imagination, a stressful situation (several times if necessary) without becoming panicky or retreating from the scene.

The person should become relaxed and comfortable in quiet surroundings, as with other relaxation techniques. Next, while relaxed, the stressful situation should be envisaged and focused on.

The feelings of anxiety or anger or disgust that develop should be held in check by breathing slowly and deeply, or actively relaxing some groups of muscles, as in progressive relaxation. Tell yourself not to worry but to work out how to cope with the situation; rehearse in the mind various ways of dealing with it. Do not select just one method of coping but think through several alternatives, and get clear in the mind the points of resistance and how much compromise is possible. Envisage the worst consequences of the situation and then assess whether it is really as bad as you had thought.

Then switch off and try to forget about it all, by concentrating on a relaxing image, such as a fine view seen on holiday. After a few minutes, the whole sequence can be repeated.

A useful variation of this method, which needs the help of someone else, is role-playing in which the person acts his own part and the helper that of the antagonist. A difficult or feared situation (such as how to say 'no') is realistically rehearsed until the stress goes out of it and, hopefully, will not come back when the scene is re-enacted in reality.

biofeedback

This method was introduced in the late '60s, as a means of facilitating relaxation and reducing anxiety, and helping the treatment of some stress-related conditions. But research evidence in the last few years has not confirmed early claims made on behalf of the therapeutic value of the technique.

It is essentially a technique which tries to make the individual aware of changes in bodily responses and functions as they happen, with the aim that he should gradually be able to control those functions. Heart rate can be monitored and recorded, so can muscle activity and sweating on the palms of the hands. The brainwaves can be recorded. 'Alpha' waves (frequency of 8 to 13 cycles per second) are associated with relaxation and well-being; 'beta' waves (14–20 cycles per second) are dominant when the person is aroused.

Biofeedback involves the use of devices which provide constant (visual or aural) information about the state of tension or relaxation. The person tries to change the reading of the machine so that the indicator will move in the right direction, or the noise stop, or whatever is the machine's indication of 'greater relaxation'—and by doing so, may be able to achieve greater relaxation.

Biofeedback machines in use in hospital departments are fairly complex, because they are used in connection with research. But small and relatively inexpensive devices are now available to the public, for use at home or anywhere else. Those for monitoring muscular tension or sweating are the simplest to operate; the sweat-measuring ones are the least expensive. There are pocket-sized instruments that look like a small transistor radio, and cost around £50 each. A person's degree of sweating, reflecting his level of tension or relaxation, is picked up by two small electrodes, attached to fingertips or the palm, and feedback information is given as a continuous tone or click, through an earphone no bigger than a hearing aid. Some people derive encouragement from seeing the success of their attempts recorded by a machine. For others, the same results might be achieved without the use of machines.

alternative medicine

It is a criticism of conventional medicine that it encourages people to rely on cures rather than to understand, and take some responsibility for, the causes of their ill health. Wonder treatments such as antibiotics, cortisone, anti-depressant drugs and intricate heart surgery have helped foster this view. Diagnosis and treatment in alternative medicine are aimed not so much at relieving symptoms as at finding and correcting ways in which the body is in conflict with its environment.

Alternative therapists (who include doctors) reckon that orthodox medicine puts too little emphasis on the many ways in which we affect our own health – diet, smoking and drinking habits, exercise, attitudes and emotions.

It is likely that if you consult someone practising alternative medicine such as homoeopathy, healing by touch, naturopathy, herbalism, osteopathy, acupuncture, he will enquire fully into how you live and will put emphasis on adjusting your lifestyle.

Critics of alternative therapies say that they work by a placebo effect – and that it is only the practitioner's interest in the patient, during generally long consultations, and his assurances that the treatment works, which cause the patient to get better. To some extent, this is what happens with conventional treatments, too.

People who are interested in any forms of alternative therapy should not feel shy of trying out methods which they think may suit them. It would be a mistake to think that any one system of treatment is the answer to all human disorders; most of us can benefit by selecting appropriate bits from different methods.

It's not all bad

Stress cannot be avoided. It is inherent in the human condition and our century has intensified many stresses and added new ones. Since it cannot be avoided, it has to be managed and coped with. First, the exact cause of stress should be identified and scrutinised because it could be that be that we are imposing some stresses unnecessarily on ourselves. Sometimes a change in attitudes could resolve the problem. Adapting to stress can bring about personal changes which are often all to the good. Other stresses, particularly not of our making, could be eased by taking definite steps such as changing jobs, or moving house or, if it has to be, getting divorced. In some cases, the only solution is to come to terms with unpleasant realities since they are there to stay and by accepting them once and for all, lessen their stressful impact.

It is important at all times to keep a positive self-image and not to indulge in self-fulfilling negative prophecies. Whenever you attempt a new way of coping with stress, whether you succeed or not, do a kind of de-briefing afterwards. Ask yourself what went well and what went wrong, how you might have handled things differently; think about it and tell yourself all the positive and useful aspects of what you did. You can learn from any experience, good or bad.

Stress is too often thought of as only bad; people fail to see that it can be a positive force in their lives. The secret, if we are to be mentally and physically as healthy as possible, is to find our optimum level of stress. This varies from person to person and also varies in ourselves from one day to the next. Each of the different areas of satisfaction in life – work, study, family, marriage, intimate and other relationships, social activities, leisure, sport – carries its own stresses. You may find that you can tolerate higher levels of stress in some areas than in others, and may even actively seek them in one or other area.

With no stress, no pressure or demands on us, it would be hard to get going at all, and many people would lack motivation. Too much stress is bad, but so is too little.

Stress checklist

warning signs

can include

increased irritability
becoming markedly more suspicious
   more fussy
   more gloomy
   more anything
indecision
unsociable behaviour
restlessness
inability to concentrate
loss of appetite
   (or overeating)
loss of interest in sex
   (or recourse to casual sex)
loss of sleep
drinking more
smoking more
worrying about all sorts of things
feeling tense
bodily symptoms such as
   headaches
   indigestion
   palpitations
   backache
   breathlessness
   nausea
   twitching
   odd aches and pains
tiredness

If you notice some of these, be aware that they may be signs of mounting stress, so try to tackle the underlying cause, not just the symptom.

identifying the source

(May be obvious – for example money worries, loss of job, bereavement.)

May lie hidden under layers of rationalisation, projection, denial.
So, try to be honest with yourself.

May be due to conflict: not wanting to do something you feel you ought to; wanting to do incompatible things; feeling ambivalent towards someone.
So, try to sort out your feelings.

May be due to feeling helpless in a particular situation.
So, try to assess realistically whether or not there is anything you can do.

May be due to a situation making you feel bad about yourself (inadequate, ignored, guilty, for example).
So, try to change your perception of the situation.

May be due to an accumulation of factors, some related, some not.
So, try to isolate them and see how they interact.

May be due to feeling pressurised, perhaps because you feel you have to prove yourself or think there is no one else to carry the load.
So, either way, try to share or shed some of it.

May be due to trying to be someone or something which is not really you.
So, ask yourself why.

May be due merely to fears of what might happen or even vague fears that you have never put into words.
So, ask yourself: fact or fiction?

some practical hints

ask yourself what is the worst thing that could happen

aim to turn your worries into problems – by definition, problems are something to be solved

come to a decision and act on it – even a 'bad' decision is likely to be less stressful than remaining in a state of indecision

rehearse beforehand how you will deal with a situation – role playing is a good way of doing this

catch a stressful situation early – before it escalates

make use of relaxation – including short spells during the day

remember how you coped before and try to do the same again – or analyse why it is not possible this time and what you can do instead

sort out what can be cured and what must be endured – and what cannot be cured but need not be endured

keep yourself as healthy as possible

cultivate (other) interests to counteract stress

have holidays and minibreaks – whenever you can

expend time and effort on human relationships – cultivate your friends and make new ones try to establish your own values and how you want to live and relate to other people

avoid making too many changes in your life all at once

give yourself recognition – so that you do not feel hurt if you do not get it from others

seek a confidant – but not just to moan about someone else: better try to express your feelings to that person directly

take sensible steps to deal with a situation and when you have done all you can, remember the lilies of the field

count your blessings once in a while

remember that it is not just how things are but also how you choose to feel about them

be your own best friend – be nice to yourself, but accept responsibility for yourself and your actions

◑ make use of any organisations that might help you – send them a stamped addressed envelope for details.

some do's . . . .

○ remember that tomorrow is another day ○ let bygones be bygones ○ opt for the bird in the hand ○ be a good neighbour ○ cultivate your garden ○ remember Kipling's *If* ○ smile ○ have a go ○ give someone a hug ○ take a deep breath (or, better still, several) ○ walk tall (physically and metaphorically) ○ count up to 10 ○ leave the ratrace to others ○ do something (bake a cake) ○ make sure your glass is half full and not half empty ○ look your best ○ have a giggle ○ save it to cool your porridge ○ walk, dance, cycle, swim ○ gather rosebuds ○ enjoy half a loaf ○ get in touch with a friend ○ listen to yourself ○ have a catnap ○ smell a flower, watch a cloud, write a poem ○ share it ○ enjoy your achievements ○ worry afterwards ○ kiss and make up ○ listen to music ○ have time to yourself ○ welcome feedback ○ be a brave coward ○ hold up your head ○ grow old gracefully ○ be thankful for small mercies ○ take time off ○ accept what people have to offer ○ be your own person

. . . and don't's

○ don't turn molehills into mountains ○ don't beat your head against a brick wall ○ don't bottle things up ○ don't always want the upper hand ○ don't jump down people's throats ○ don't blame it all on your parents, husband, wife, neighbour, cat ○ don't wish you were someone else ○ don't underestimate yourself ○ don't be too busy to have time for people ○ don't refuse to listen ○ don't look for trouble ○ don't sigh ○ don't tear you hair (or you'll have an extra problem) ○ don't let the sun go down upon your wrath ○ don't be so sure the grass is greener ○ don't stick your head in the sand ○ don't tilt at windmills ○ don't expect life to be fair ○ don't expect to reform anyone ○ don't lose sleep over it ○ don't despair ○ don't feel it's too late.

Index

Index

Avoiding heart trouble

identifies the factors which make a person more likely to develop heart trouble and describes how the various risk factors interact: cigarette smoking, raised blood pressure, high level of blood fats, stress, hereditary and dietary factors, oral contraceptives, overweight. It warns of the more serious signs and symptoms of heart trouble and, where possible, tells you what can be done about them.

Living through middle age

is a book for people between the ages of 40 and 60. It gives sound advice on how to take care of yourself at this difficult time when the body is going through many physical changes. It tells you how to minimise any adverse effects such as problems with hair, skin and teeth, and also advises on health risks, such as being overweight. It includes a section on the menopause, and on psychological problems for both men and women—such as depression and the difficulties of sexual adjustment at this time.

Getting a new job

is a practical guide to the steps to take from when one job ends to the day the next one begins. The circumstances relating to unfair dismissal are explained and the remedies available. The book defines redundancy and lists your rights; it explains how redundancy payment is calculated and what can be done when an employer does not pay up. It also suggests how an employer can help a redundant employee find another job.

The book deals with job hunting, how to apply, what to do to get an interview and making sure that the interview goes well. The book deals with the points to consider when being offered a job and what is involved as an employee and as an employer—the legal rights and obligations on both sides.

Which? way to buy, sell and move house

takes you through all the stages of moving to another home—considers the pros and cons of different places; house hunting, viewing, having a survey; making an offer, getting a mortgage, completing the purchase, selling the present home. It explains the legal procedures and the likely costs. Buying and selling at an auction and in Scotland are specifically dealt with. The practical arrangements for the move and for any repairs or improvements to the new house are described. Advice is given for easing the tasks of sorting, packing and moving possessions, people and pets, with a removal firm or by doing it yourself, and for making the day of the move go smoothly.

The legal side of buying a house

will guide you step by step through the purchase of an owner-occupied house with a registered title in England or Wales (not Scotland). It explains what is involved when doing your own conveyancing—from obtaining and dealing with all the relevant forms, the role of the Land Registry, and the part played by local authority, building society, estate agent, surveyor to the all-important moment of exchange of contracts and, finally, completion. The book also deals with the legally less complicated procedure of selling your house.

Starting your own business

is a competent guide to the best way of making a success of a new venture. It leads the way from the first essential step—defining exactly what product or skill you have to offer—to warnings of pitfalls and difficulties. It deals with sources of capital, how to raise it, legal requirements, pricing the product, marketing and selling, premises, keeping accounts and other records, VAT and other taxes, staff relations, insurance, thinking about computers. Sources of advice and information for the small businessman are given throughout the book.

Securing your home

should help you keep burglars and car thieves at bay by telling you how to protect your home and safeguard your car. It gives practical advice on making it difficult for the burglar to get in; locks and grilles, burglar alarms, and general safety are all dealt with. And it tells you what to do and what not to do if a burglar has broken into your home or car, and how to make a claim on your insurance.

Divorce—legal procedures and financial facts

explains the financial facts to be faced when a marriage ends in divorce. It includes getting legal advice, legal aid and its drawbacks, the various orders the court can make. Fictitious case histories illustrate different situations and alternative solutions.

Dealing with household emergencies

is written for the un-handy householder who needs basic facts about simple action to take when a sudden emergency occurs. It gives advice on electrical failure, blocked drains and pipes, broken window cords and panes, stains, outbreak of fire, infestation by pests; and has a section on first aid and on making an insurance claim after an accident or damage.

Avoiding back trouble

explains how the spine is constructed and how not to stress it in everyday activities such as housework, driving, lifting and carrying, gardening, sitting. It describes symptoms of back trouble and advises on how to cope with an acute attack of back pain. It tells what to expect when examined by specialists (including the diagnostic terms that may be used) and the treatments that may be prescribed. The book ends with suggestions about how to avoid becoming a chronic back sufferer.

Which? way to slim

provides sensible advice and information for the would-be slimmer, sorting out fact from fallacy and appraising every aspect of the slimming problem. It discusses suitable weight ranges, target weights, the different methods of dieting, exercise, slimming clubs and aids. The book highlights the danger of being overweight, particularly the risk in specific circumstances: during pregnancy, in middle age, when giving up smoking. It includes weight tables, Calorie and carbohydrate charts, recipes and menus, food values, and gives encouraging advice about how to stay slim.

Pregnancy month by month

tells in detail what a pregnant women can expect at each stage of antenatal care. The book discusses where to have a baby, and compares hospital, GP maternity unit, nursing home and home confinement. It gives reasons for the various tests and examinations at antenatal clinics, and tells how to deal with the minor ailments that often accompany pregnancy. Sections on genetic counselling, having twins, claiming maternity benefits, fertility problems, contraception, abortion and provisions for unmarried mothers are also included.

The newborn baby

concentrates on the health and welfare of a new baby and reassures the mother about what is usual and normal in a baby's development. It deals primarily with the first weeks after the baby is born but there is also plenty of information about feeding and development in the following weeks and months. There are sections dealing with problems such as prematurity and the rhesus factor and descriptions of routine tests. There is advice about when to seek help from midwife, health visitor, clinic doctor or general practitioner.

Earning money at home

is for a person who has to stay at home and would like to make some money at the same time. The book explains what this entails in the way of organising domestic life, family and children, keeping accounts, taking out insurance, coping with tax, costing, dealing with customers, getting supplies. It suggests many activities that could be undertaken, with or without previous experience.

Householders action guide

deals with problems and decisions a householder may have to face, and what actions he should take to assert his rights and fulfil his obligations. It explains the rights and duties of the local authority towards the householder, and yours to them; it deals with rates and how to appeal against an assessment. Other topics include legal liability towards visitors, trespassers and casual passers-by; determining the exact location of boundaries, recognising structural and maintenance faults, employing a builder, obtaining planning permission, how to deal with nuisance caused by other people's children, their animals, noise in the street or from the flat next-door, how to avoid disputes with neighbours and, if unavoidable, what action to take.

Wills and probate

emphasises the advisability of making a will, explains how to prepare one, sign it and have it witnessed. It explains what would happen on an intestacy, that is dying without a will, and warns that a person's property may reach unforeseen beneficiaries (including the crown). It gives examples of different types of wills showing consideration for the effects of capital transfer tax. The section about probate deals in detail with the administration of an estate without a solicitor, and illustrates the various situations and problems that might arise.

What to do when someone dies

explains factually and in detail all that may need to be done: getting a doctor's certificate, reporting a death to the coroner, registering a death and getting various death certificates. Differences between burial and cremation procedure are discussed, and the arrangements that have to be made, mainly through the undertaker, for the funeral. The book details the various national insurance benefits that may be claimed.

Where to live after retirement

tackles the difficult subject of a suitable place to live in old age. The book offers practical advice on the decision whether to move or to stay put and adapt the present home to be easier to live in. It weighs up the pros and cons of the alternatives open to an older person, and the financial aspects involved, considers sheltered housing and granny flats, the problems of living in someone else's household, and residential homes.

Consumer Publications are available from Consumers' Association, Castlemead, Gascoyne Way, Hertford SG14 1LH and from booksellers.